AF260505

Love is Love:
A Woven Celtic Knot

Nacho Grandma's Quilts

Raymond K. Houston

Blue Dragon Publishing

Love is Love: A Woven Celtic Knot

by Raymond K. Houston

All rights reserved.

Published by Blue Dragon Publishing, LLC

Williamsburg, VA

www.BlueDragonPublishing.com

Copyright 2020 Raymond K. Houston

ISBN 978-1-939696-59-5 (paperback)

ISBN 978-1-939696-60-1 (eBook)

Library of Congress Control Number: 2020901166

Printed in the U.S.A.

CRA031000 Crafts & Hobbies / Quilts & Quilting

CRA061000 Crafts & Hobbies / Fiber Arts & Textiles

Cover art "Love is Love" copyright 2019 Raymond K. Houston

In private collection of Marjie Baker Kennedy.

Back cover "Love is Blue" copyright 2019 Raymond K. Houston

No part of this product may be reproduced in any form, unless otherwise stated, in which case reproduction is limited to the use of the purchaser. Permission is granted to photocopy the templates for the personal use of the retail purchaser.

The information presented in this book is presented in good faith, but no warranty is given, nor results guaranteed. Since the Author or Blue Dragon Publishing, LLC has no control over choice of materials or procedures, the Author and Publisher assume no responsibility for the use of this information.

For your convenience, we post an up-to-date listing of corrections on our website (www.BlueDragonPublishing.com). If a correction is not already noted, please email us at info@bluedragonpublishing.com.

To Joe

Table of Contents

Introduction

In June 2019, I created a quilt I titled "Love is Love" (shown on front cover). The quilt displays Celtic knots with the shape of a heart in them. "Love is Love" was juried into The Rocky Mountain Quilt Museum's fifteenth biennial exhibit of quilts made by men, "The Boys are Back in Town!" held January 20 through April 25, 2020. The quilt was only the beginning.

I experimented with dividing a long Celtic knot path into smaller sections to weave together. These are my results. The technique works with either fabric or paper. I am going to show how to trace, transfer, and weave the knot a number of ways.

The Celtic knot shown throughout this book consists of two paths: Path A and Path B.

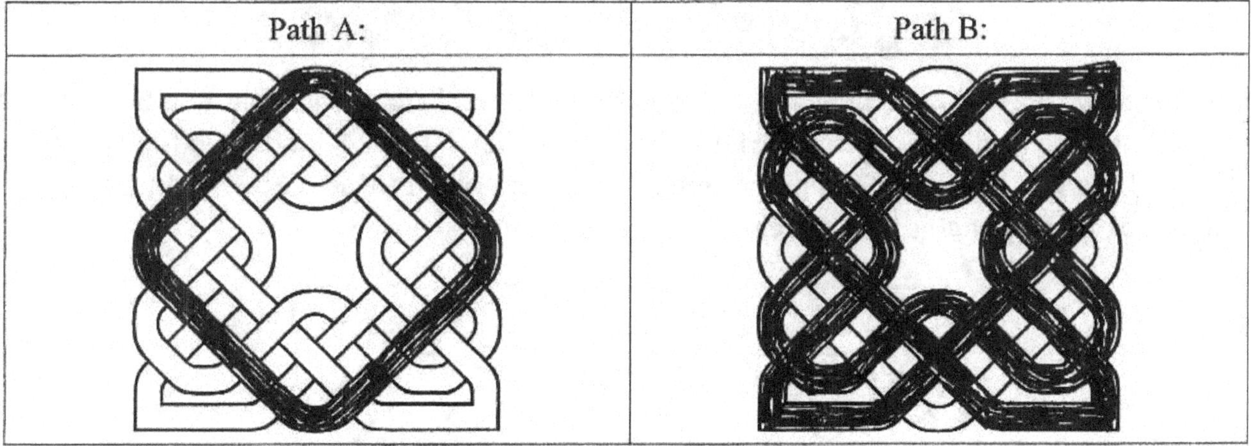

Path A is a simple loop going around and around. I can cut it from a single piece of fabric.

Path B is far from simple. The path weaves over and under itself 32 times. I can cut the outline of the path from a single piece of fabric.

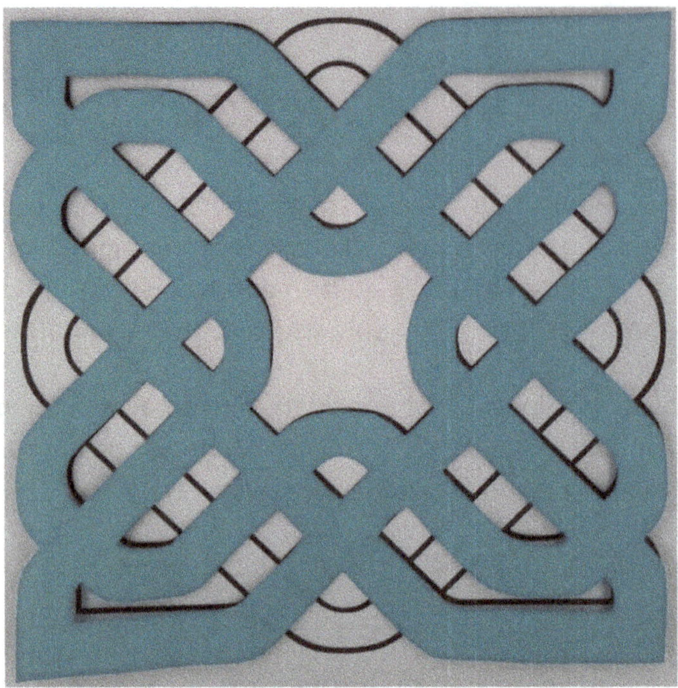

In order to weave this knot, I have to divide Path B into smaller sections that don't cross over themselves. I divided Path B into individual pieces numbered 1 to 24, starting in the lower left corner of the knot and proceeding clockwise. I am going to join these pieces, end-to-end, into sections of varying lengths before weaving them together.

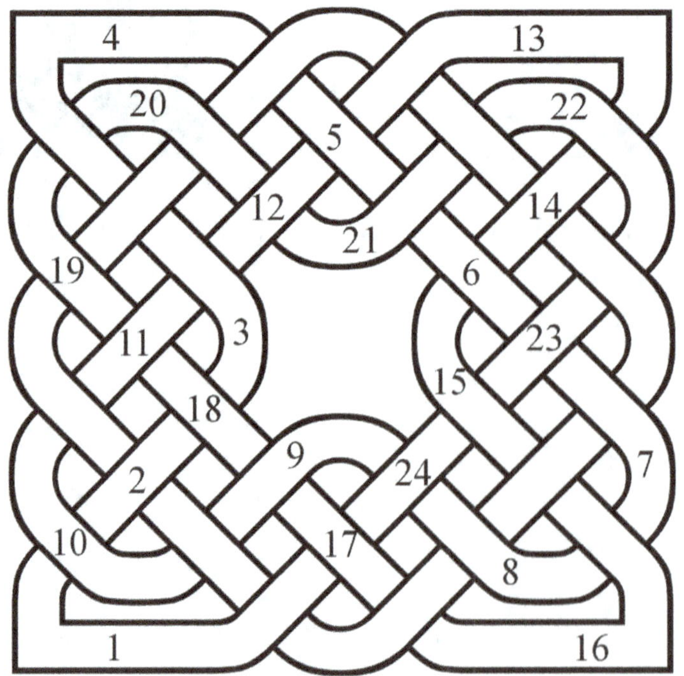

The Basics

To make these Celtic knots from fabric, you will need:

- 7" x 7" squares of paper-backed fusible web
- A pencil, pen or marker for tracing
- Scissors or a rotary cutter and cutting mat
- Iron and ironing surface
- Long, thin straight pins
- 7" x 7" squares of fabrics
- Fabric for background
- Sewing machine

To make these Celtic knots from paper, you will need:

- Colored paper
- Scissors or a rotary cutter and mat
- Paper clips, glue or stapler and staples
- Copier

1. Trace

For fabric, use the tracing template to trace the paths and path sections on separate squares of paper-backed fusible web, paper side up. When tracing Path B pieces, extend the cut ends no longer than the width of the path above.

For paper, copy the tracing template on colored paper and cut the paths and path sections from it. When cutting Path B pieces, extend the cut ends no longer than the width of the path above.

2. Transfer

For fabric, press the traced paths, adhesive side down, to the reverse side of fabric squares according to the manufacturer's instructions.

Trim the paths along both edges. Remove the paper backing.

3. Weave

Note: tracing and transferring the paths to fabric reverses the direction the paths face. Pieces and path sections traced on the left half of the knot are positioned on the right half of the knot, and vice versa. This cannot be avoided.

Paper paths can be woven face up or face down. They are shown face down throughout.

Use the placement guide to position the paths for weaving (use the tracing template to position face-up paper paths). You need to pin the fabric paths together as you weave them to stabilize the knot. You need to glue or staple the paper paths together for the same reason.

The rule of thumb is when a path crosses over another path (even itself), it crosses under the next path it encounters (and vice versa). After weaving, make sure the over and under sequence is correct for both paths.

Unpin the fabric paths from the placement guide, but keep the paths pinned together, so the entire knot moves freely and acts as a single unit.

Position the fabric knot on the background fabric, adhesive side down. Starting along the bottom or top of the knot, remove the pins and press the knot to the background fabric, row by row.

Stitch the two paths to the background fabric as desired.

Loosen the paper paths from the placement guide, but keep the paths fastened together, so the entire knot moves freely and acts as a single unit.

Position and attach the paper knot on a background as desired.

Different Looks

The Path B sections are fluid. Here, I used the same numbering throughout, starting with "1" in the lower left corner and proceeding clockwise. I can also designate a different piece of Path B as "1," and proceed clockwise, to get slightly different results.

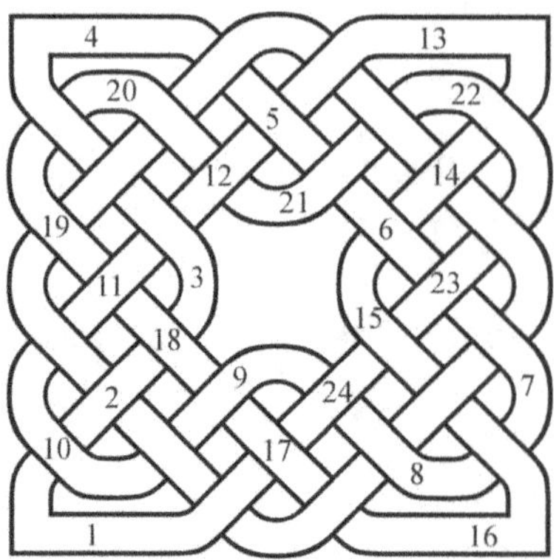

Here are three variations on a simple division. The first variation starts with piece #1; the second variation starts with piece #2; the third variation starts with piece #4.

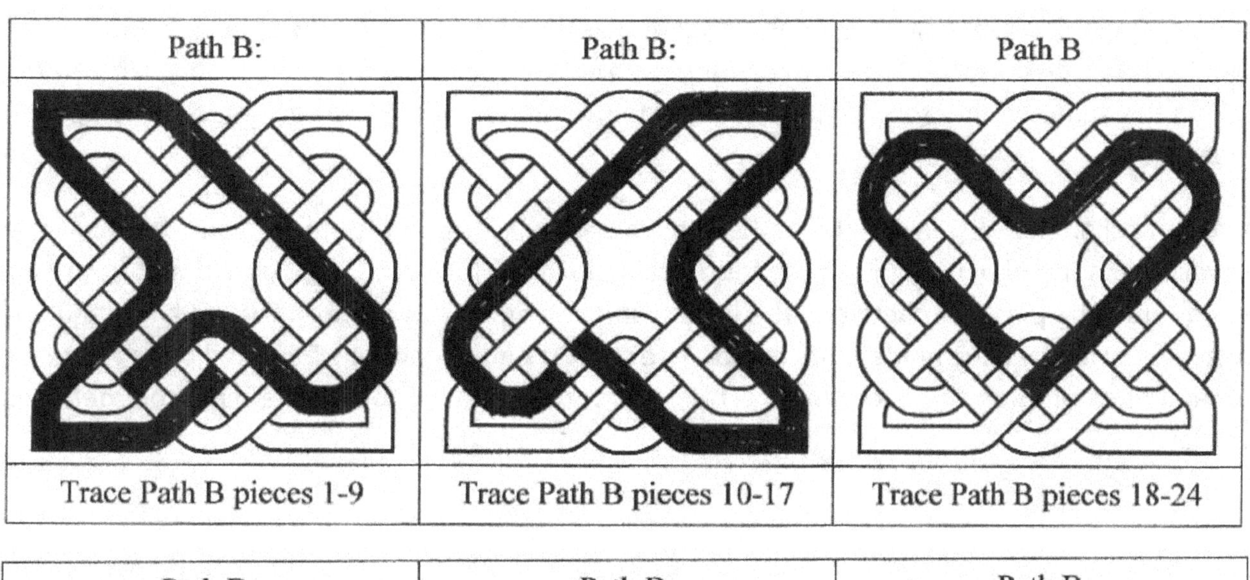

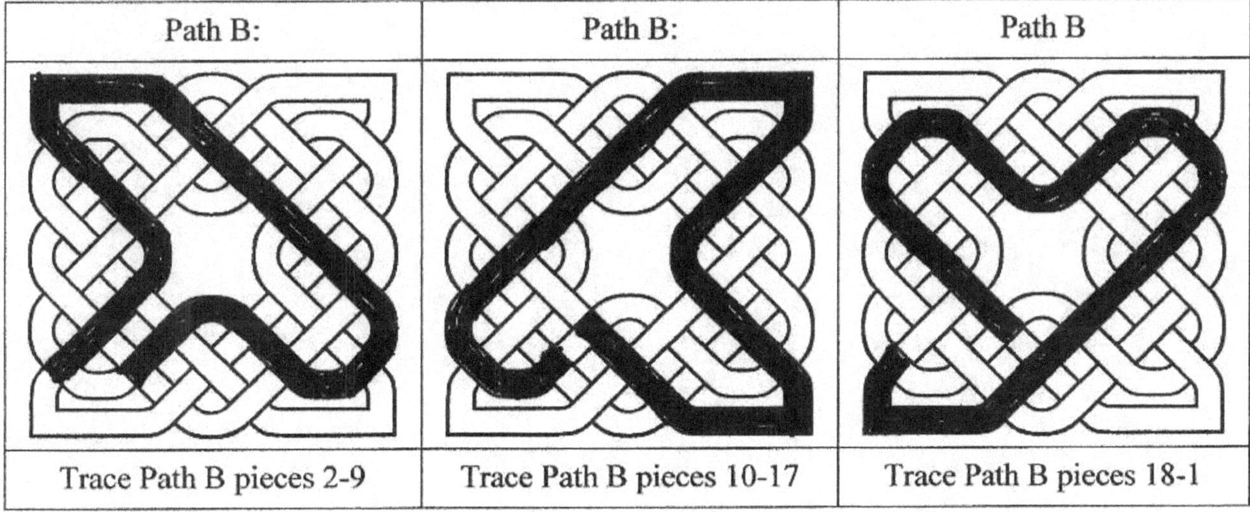

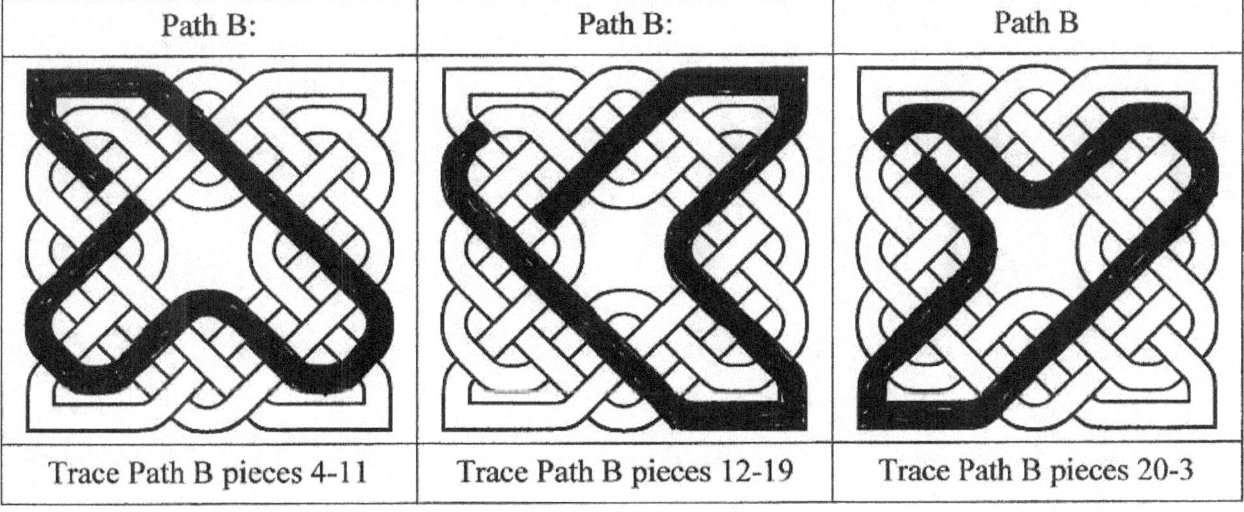

Lessons Learned

When I first began doing Celtic knots in 2011, I traced the shapes with the adhesive side up, so the paths wouldn't reverse directions. I abandoned the idea for several reasons: a pencil or pen would sometimes scratch or tear the adhesive from the paper while tracing; and a felt pen left ink on the adhesive that showed through light fabrics unless trimmed away. "Reverse happens," I learned.

I do not recommend weaving the paths with the adhesive side up because you would have to cover the knot with your background fabric, face down, before pressing. You would be working blind removing pins from between the layers; and you won't see the front of the knot (and any mistakes you may have made) until it's too late to fix them. It would be best to flip the knot face up and position it on the background fabric, but you'll still have to remove pins from between the layers.

Celtic Knot #1

I divided Path B into three unequal sections that don't cross themselves (only each other).

Trace the outline of Path A.
Trace Path B, pieces 1 to 9.
Trace Path B, pieces 10 to 17.
Trace Path B, pieces 18 to 24.

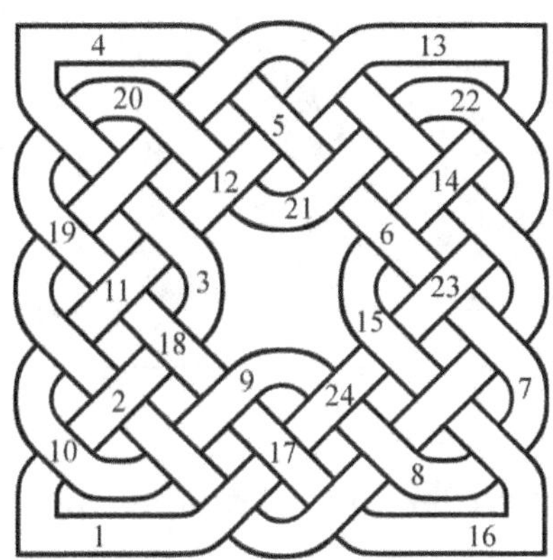

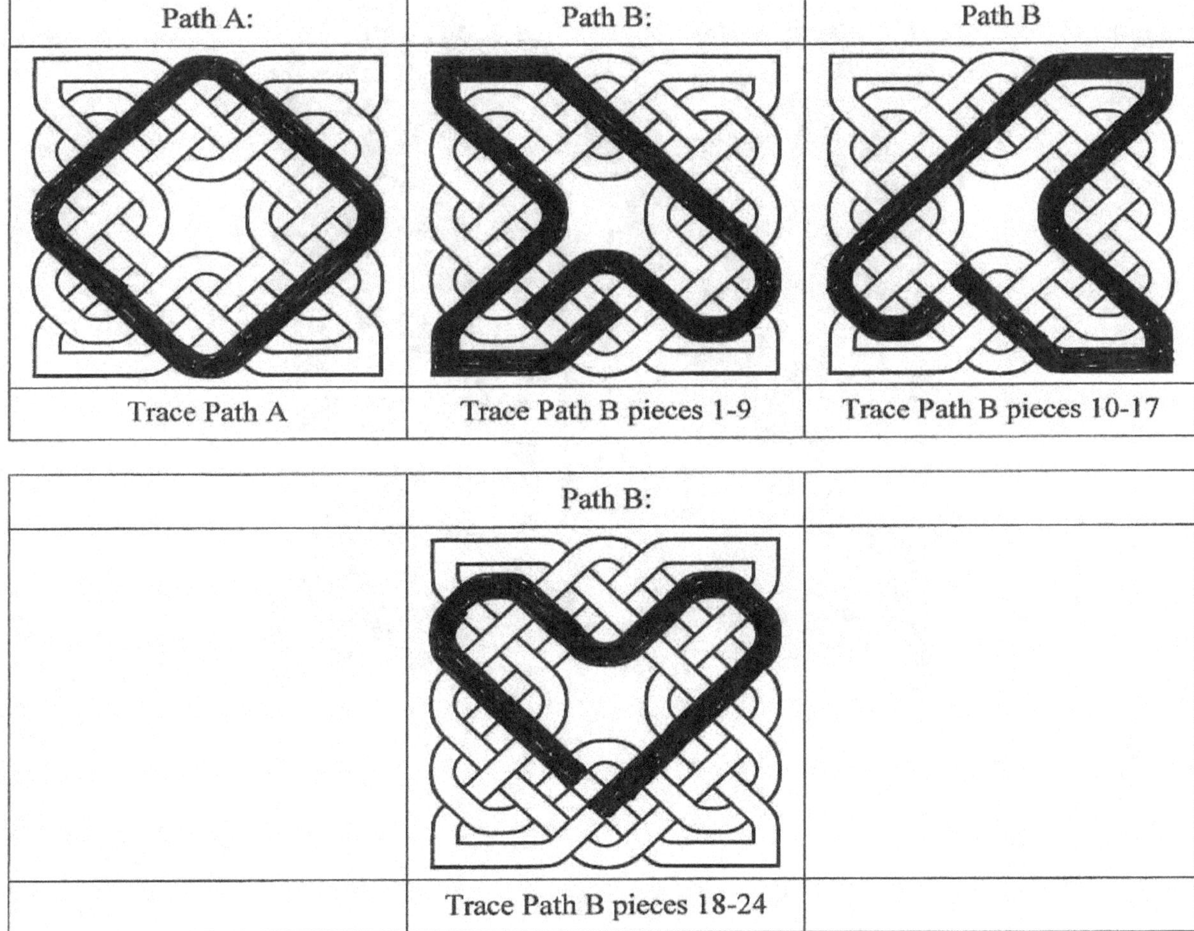

Path A:	Path B:	Path B
Trace Path A	Trace Path B pieces 1-9	Trace Path B pieces 10-17

	Path B:	
	Trace Path B pieces 18-24	

1. Rotate the sections 180 degrees, so the cut ends are at the top of the knot.

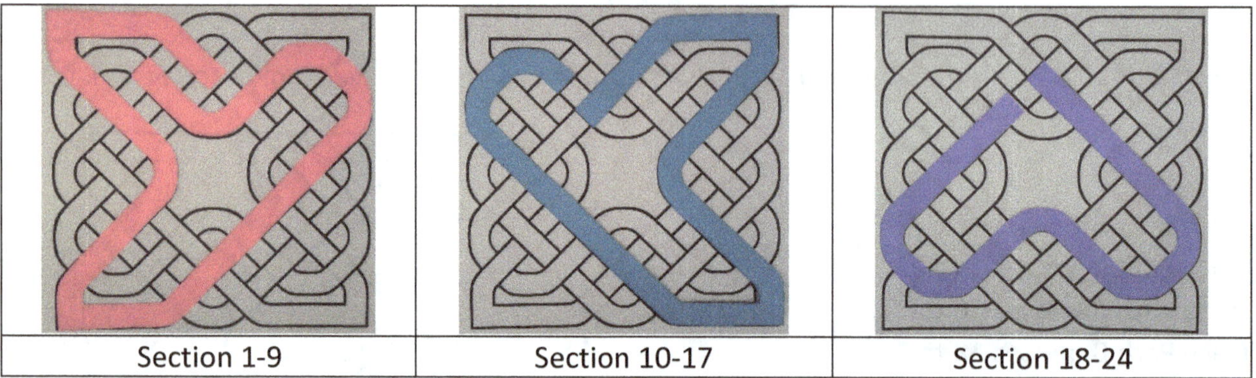

<table>
<tr><td>Section 1-9</td><td>Section 10-17</td><td>Section 18-24</td></tr>
</table>

2. Position Section 1-9 on the placement guide; position Path A on top of Section 1-9; position Section 10-17 on top of Path A. Fasten the path intersections to the placement guide along the bottom of the knot to anchor them in place where indicated.

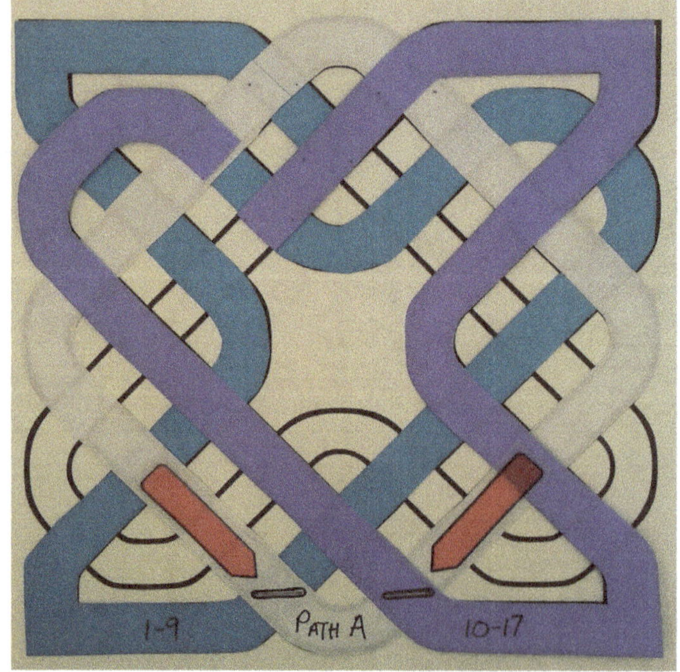

3. At the top of the knot, cut Path A where indicated (the cut ends are tucked under later).

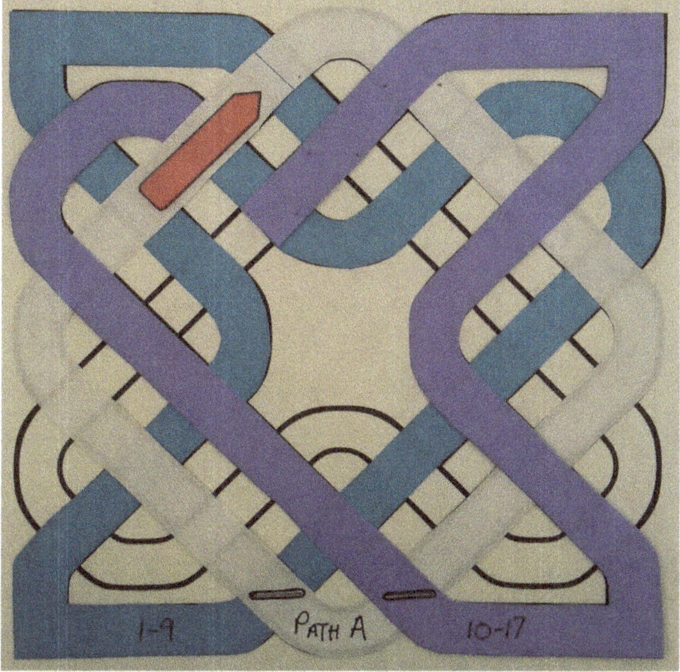

4. Lift left end of Section 10-17 and right end of Section 1-9 out of the way. Lay down Section 10-17, and then Section 1-9. Fasten path intersection where indicated.

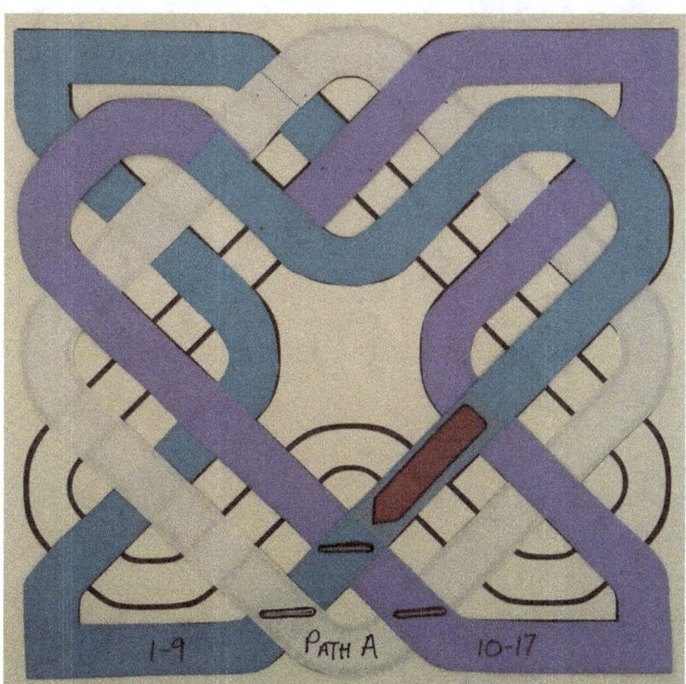

5. Lift left ends of Sections 1-9, 10-17, and right end of Path A out of the way. Position Section 18-24 on the placement guide. Lay down left ends of Sections 1-9, 10-17, and right end of Path A. Fasten path intersections where indicated.

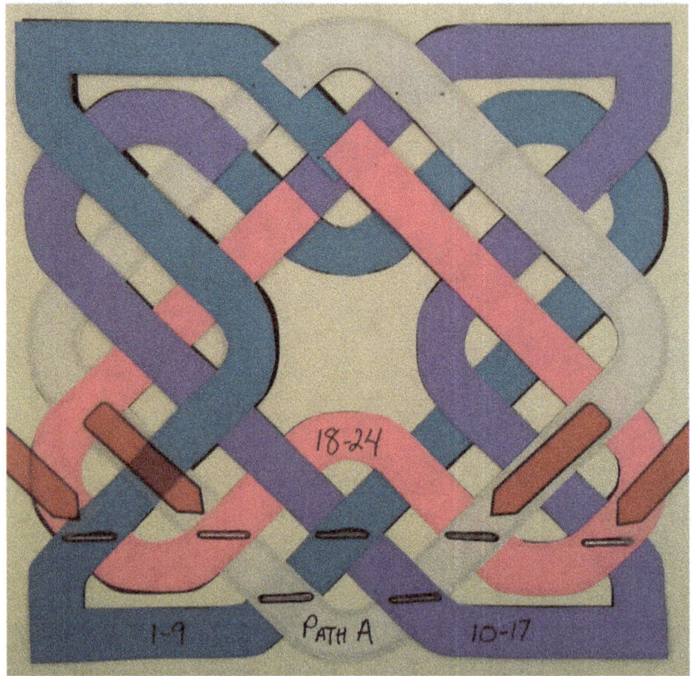

6. Lift left ends of Sections 1-9, 18-24, and Path A out of the way. Lay down Section 1-9, then Path A, and then Section 18-24. Fasten path intersections where indicated.

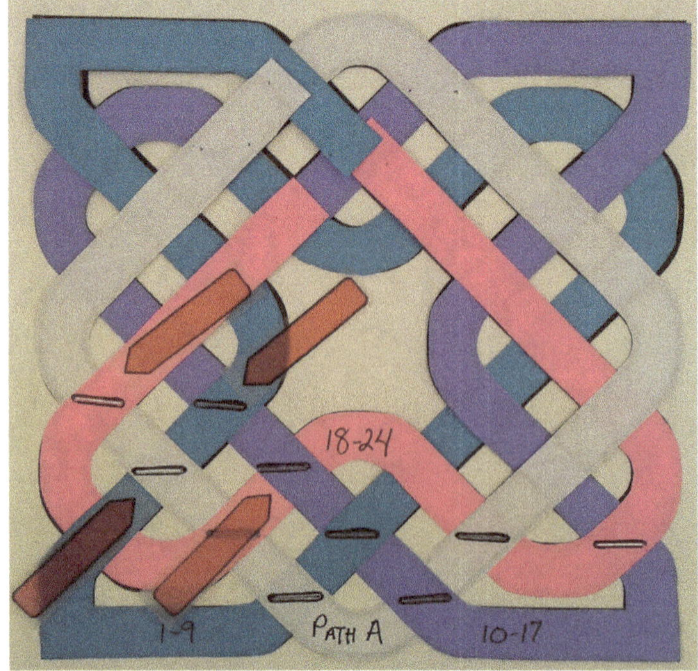

7. Lift left ends of Sections 1-9, 10-17, 18-24, and Path A out of the way. Lay down Section 1-9, then Section 18-24, then Section 10-17, and then Path A. Fasten path intersections where indicated.

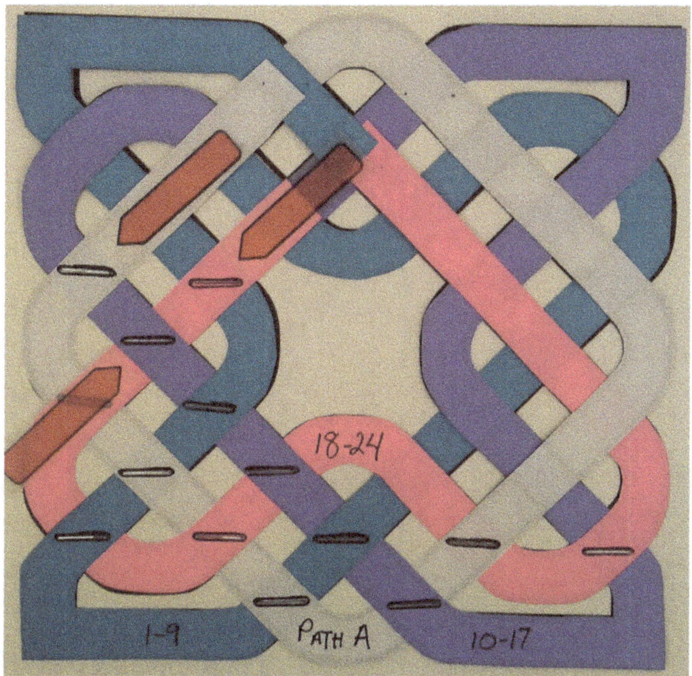

8. Lift left ends of Sections 1-9, 10-17, and Path A out of the way. Lay down Path A, then Section 1-9, and then Section 10-17. Tuck the left end of section 10-17 under Path A. Fasten path intersections where indicated.

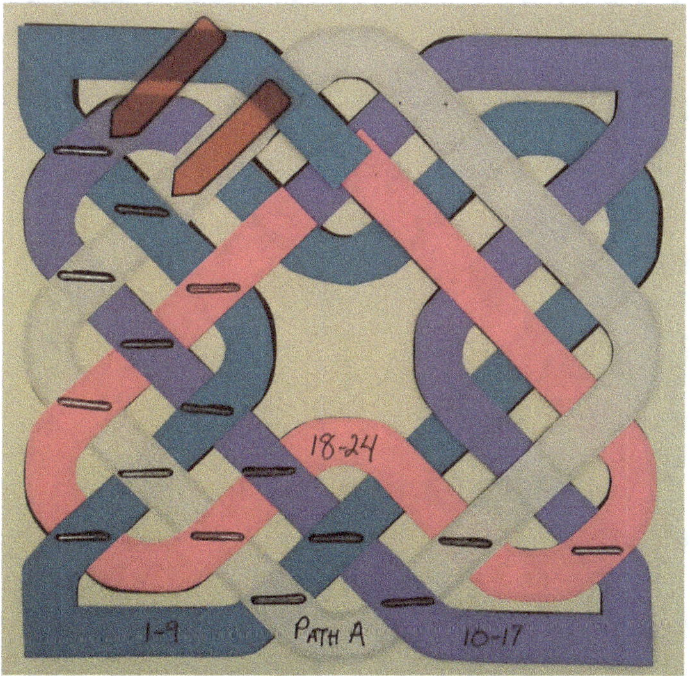

9. Lift right ends of Sections 1-9, 10-17, 18-24, and Path A out of the way. Lay down Section 18-24, then Path A, then Section 10-17, and then Section 1-9. Fasten path intersections where indicated.

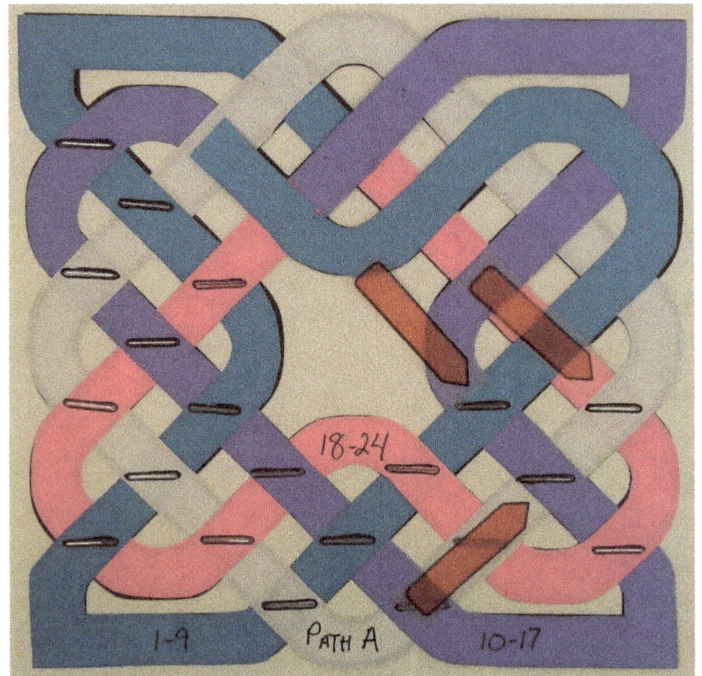

10. Lift right ends of Sections 1-9, 10-17, 18-24, and Path A out of the way. Lay down Path A, then Section 1-9, then Section 18-24, and then Section 10-17. Fasten path intersections where indicated.

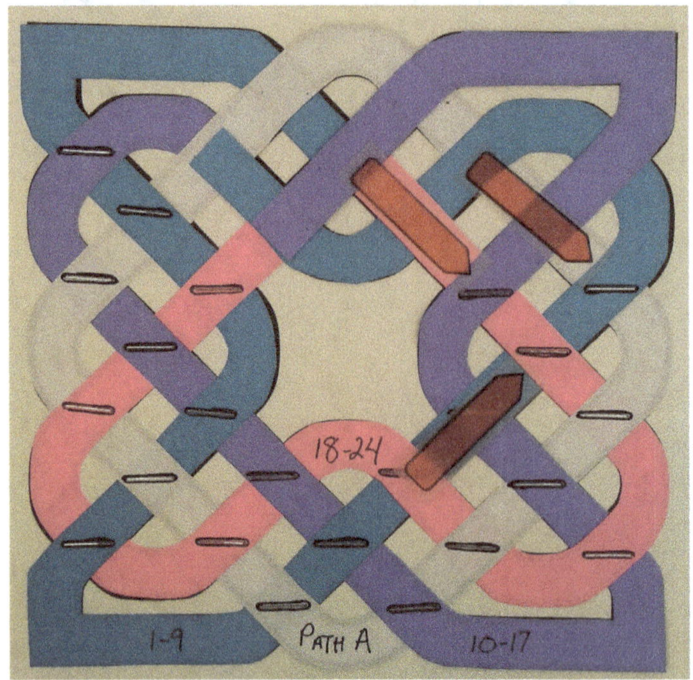

11. Lift right ends of Section 10-17, and Path A out of the way. Lay down Section 10-17, and then Path A. Fasten path intersections where indicated.

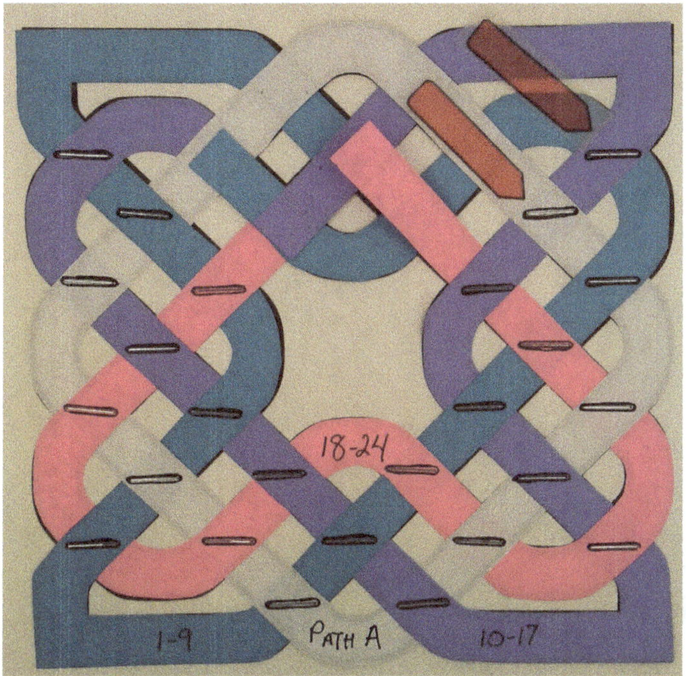

12. Lift right ends of Sections 1-9, 18-24, and Path A out of the way. Lay down Path A, then Section 1-9, and then Section 18-24. Tuck the left end of Section 18-24 under Section 10-17. Fasten path intersections where indicated.

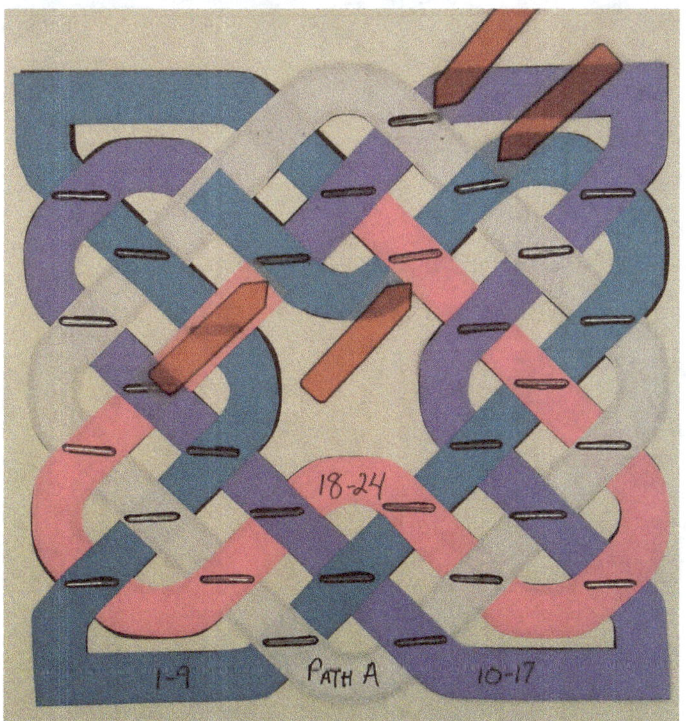

13. Tuck the right end of Section 1-9 under Path A. Tuck the ends of Path A under Section 1-9.
Fasten path intersections where indicated.

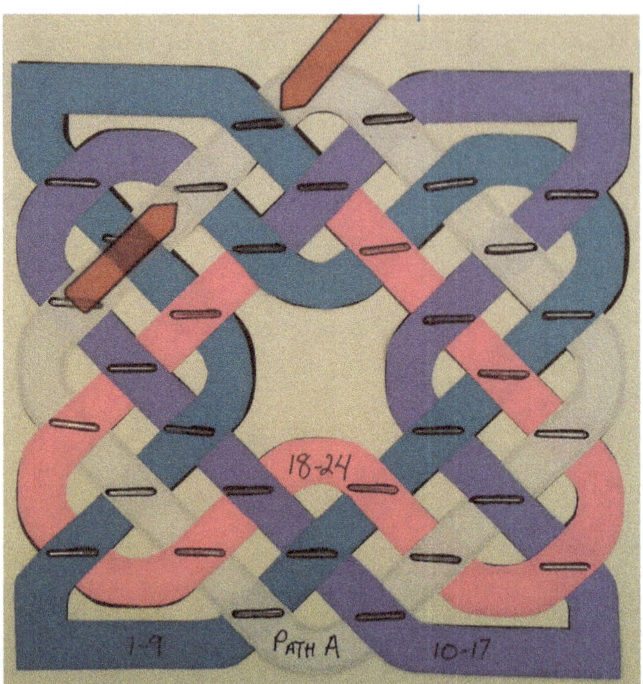

14. Rotate the knot to reveal an open-bottom heart.

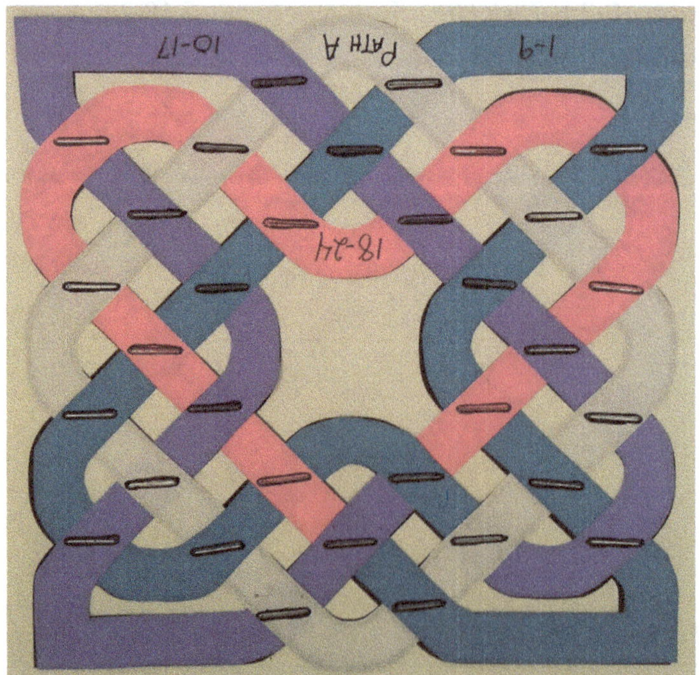

Celtic Knot #2

I divided Path B into equal halves; they are the identical shape. I further divided the halves so the sections wouldn't cross themselves.

Trace the outline of Path A.
Trace Path B, pieces 1 to 9.
Trace Path B, pieces 10 to 12.
Trace Path B, pieces 13 to 21.
Trace Path B, pieces 22 to 24.

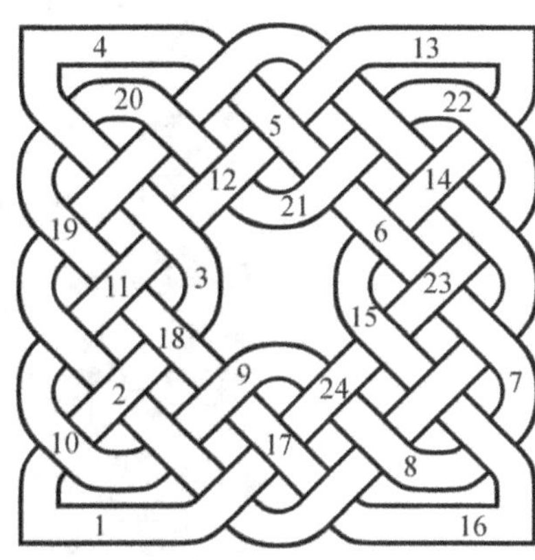

Path A:	Path B:	Path B
Trace Path A	Trace Path B pieces 1-9	Trace Path B pieces 10-12

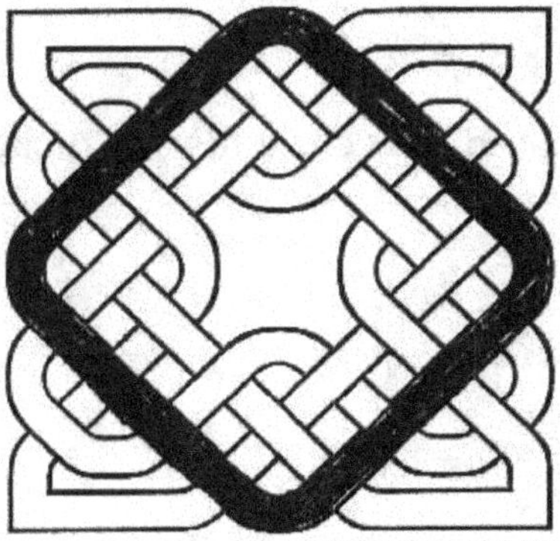

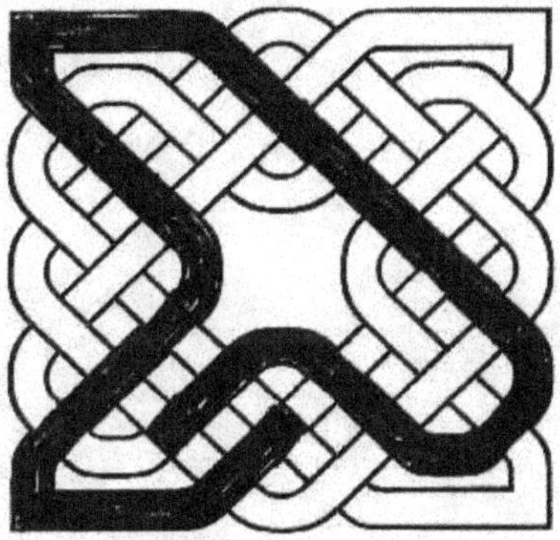

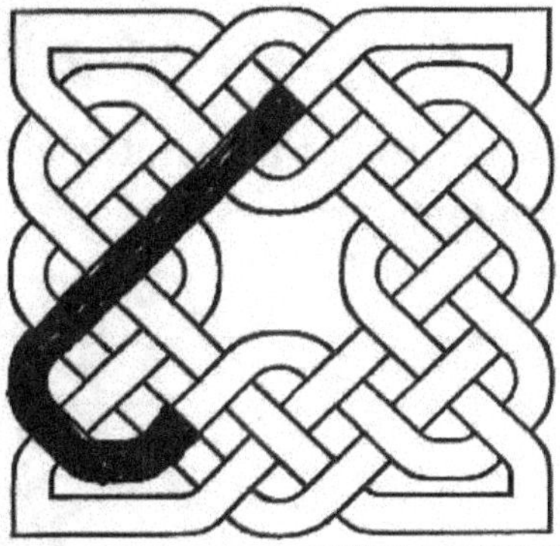

	Path B:	Path B
	Trace Path B pieces 13-21	Trace Path B pieces 22-24

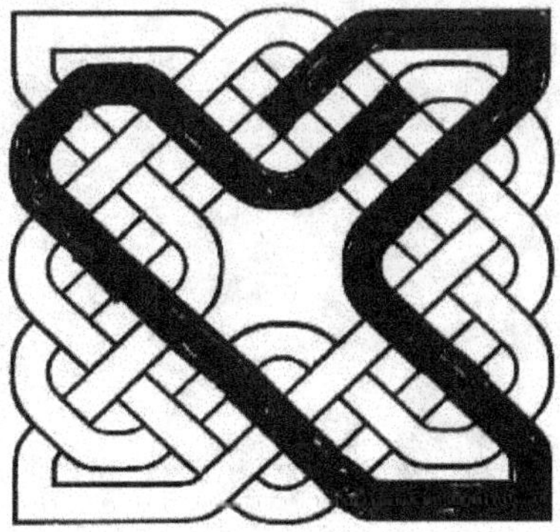

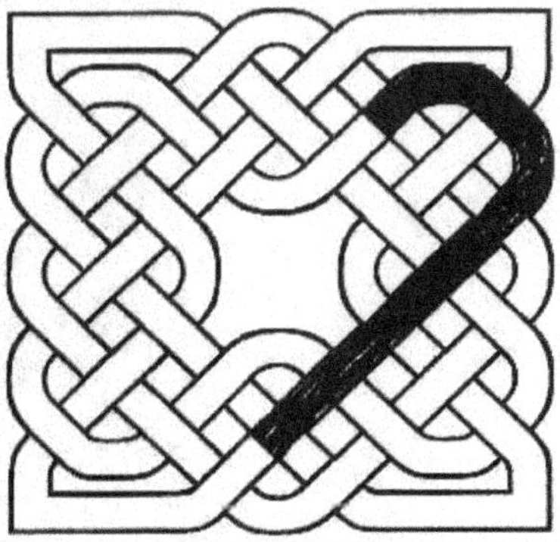

1. Position Section 13-21 on the placement guide; position Path A on top of Section 13-21; position Section 1-9 on top of Path A. Fasten the path intersections to the placement guide along the bottom of the knot to anchor them in place where indicated.

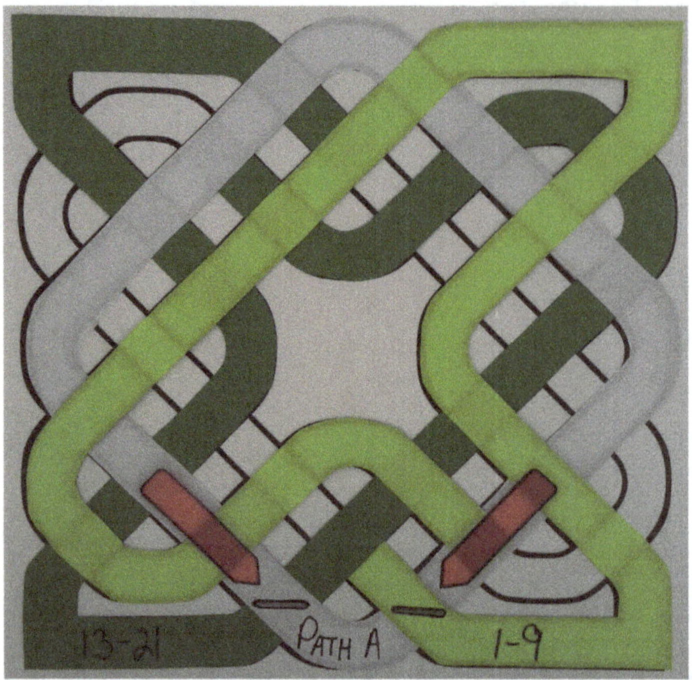

2. At the top of the knot, cut Path A and Section 1-9 where indicated (the cut ends are tucked under later).

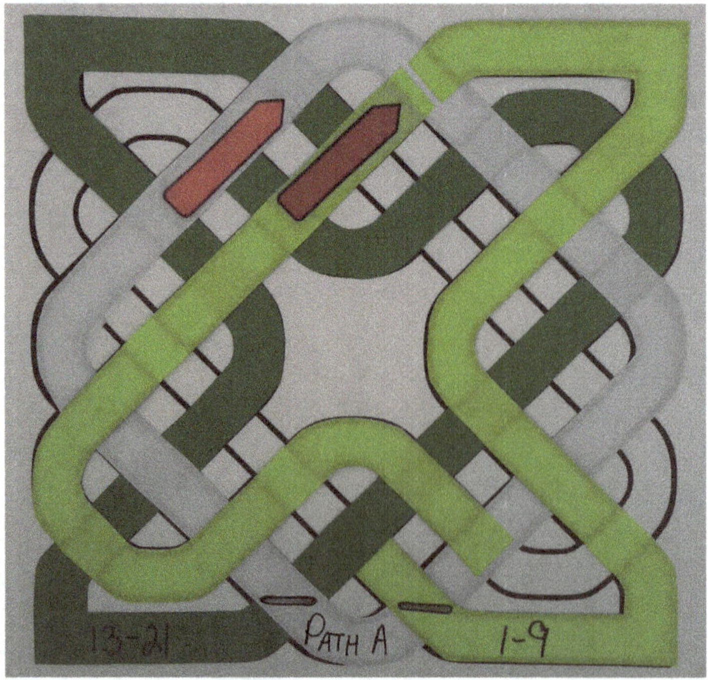

3. Lift right ends of Section 13-21, and Path A out of the way. Position Section 22-24 on the placement guide. Lay down Section 13-21 and Path A. Fasten path intersections where indicated.

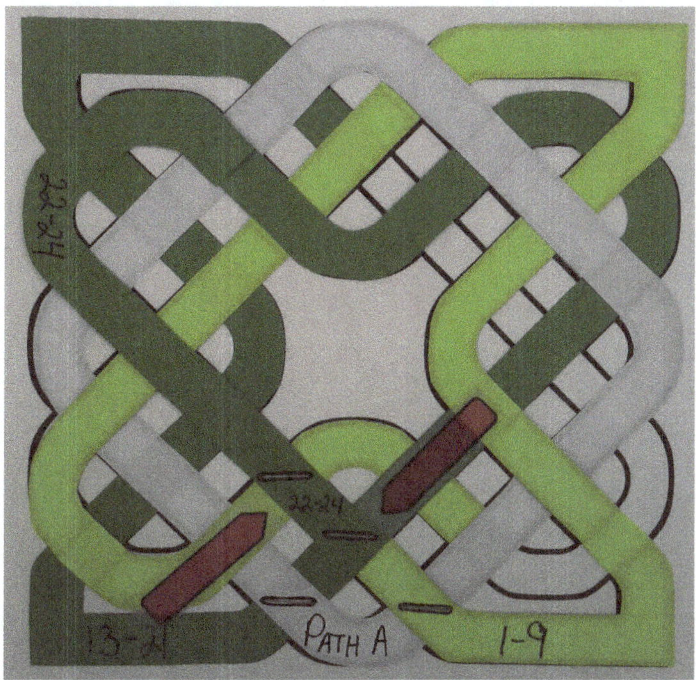

4. Lift left ends of Sections 1-9, 13-21, 22-24, and Path A out of the way. Lay down Path A, then Section 1-9, and then Section 13-21. Fasten path intersections where indicated.

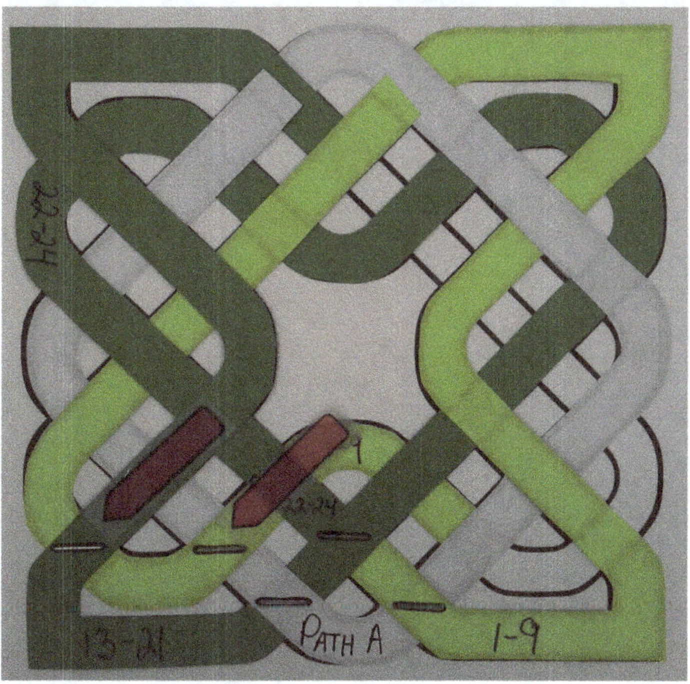

5. Lift left ends of Sections 1-9, 13-21, 22-24, and Path A out of the way. Lay down Section 22-24, then Section 13-21, then Path A, and then Section 1-9. Fasten path intersections where indicated.

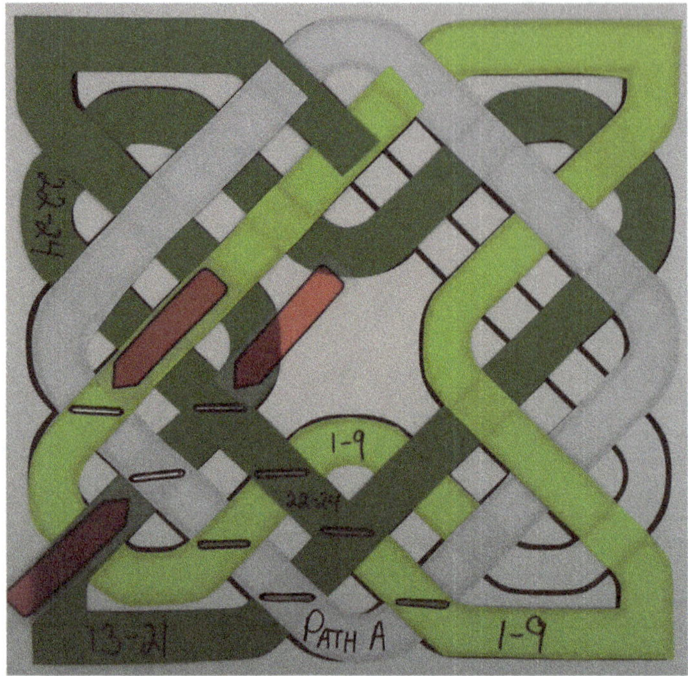

6. Lift left ends of Sections 1-9, 22-24, and Path A out of the way. Lay down Section 1-9, then Section 22-24, and then Path A. Fasten path intersections where indicated.

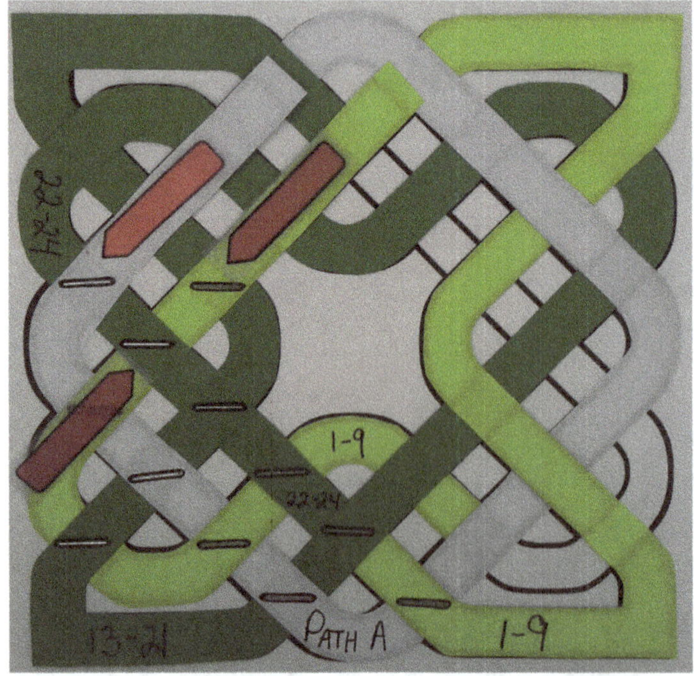

7. Lift left ends of Sections 13-21, 22-24, and Path A out of the way. Lay down Path A, then Section 13-21, and then Section 22-24. Tuck end of Section 22-24 under Path A. Fasten path intersections where indicated.

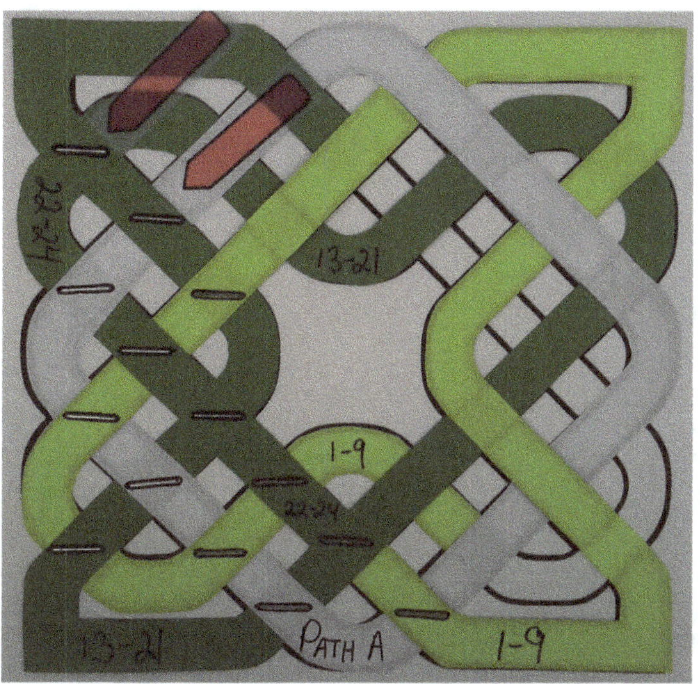

8. Lift left end of Section 1-9, and right ends of Section 13-21, and Path A out of the way. Position Section 10-12 on the placement guide. Lay down Section 13-21, then left end of Section 1-9, and then Path A. Fasten path intersections where indicated.

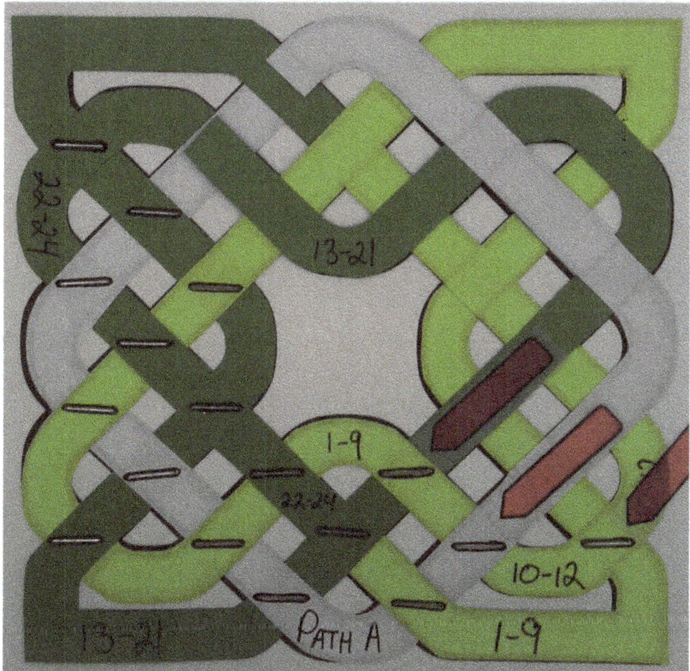

9. Lift right ends of Sections 1-9, 10-12, 13-21, and Path A out of the way. Lay down Section 10-12, then Path A, then Section 1-9, and then Section 13-21. Fasten path intersections where indicated.

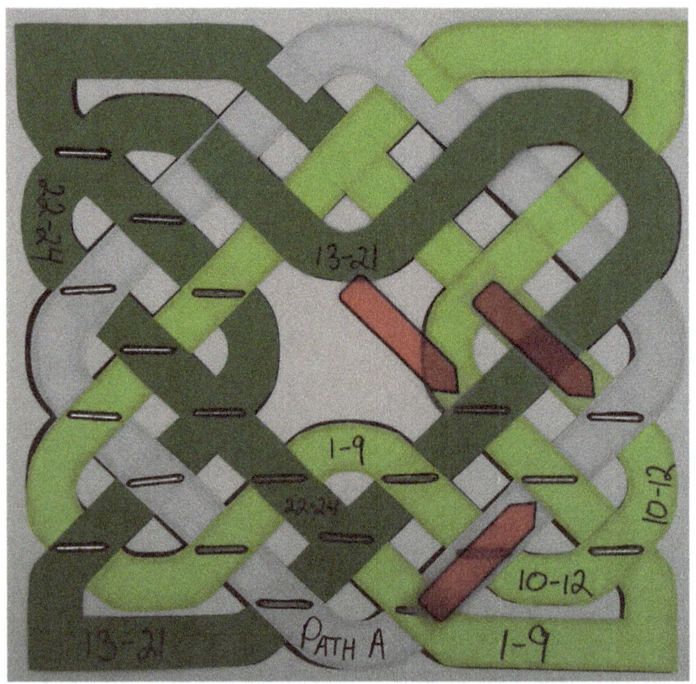

10. Lift right ends of Sections 1-9, 10-12, and 13-21 out of the way. Lay down Section 13-21, then Section 10-12, and then Section 1-9. Fasten path intersections where indicated.

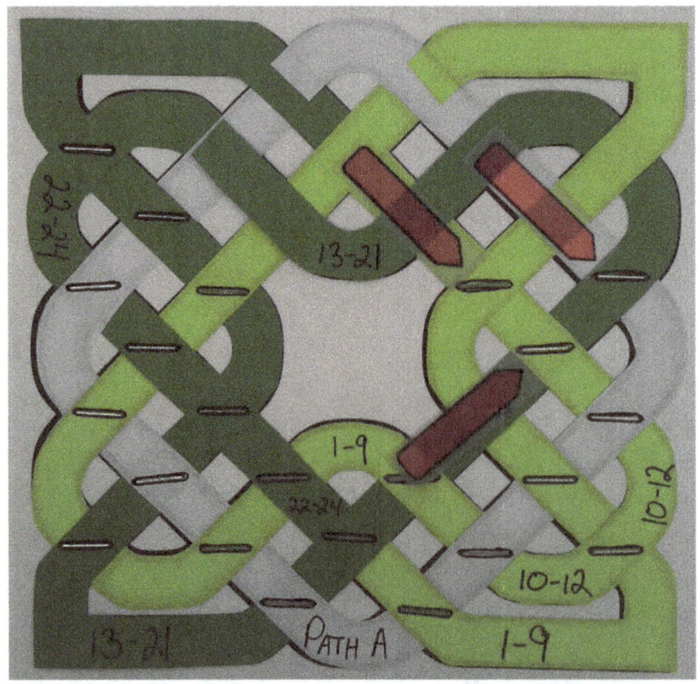

11. Lift right ends of Section 10-12, and Path A out of the way. Lay down Section 1-9, and then Path A. Fasten path intersections where indicated.

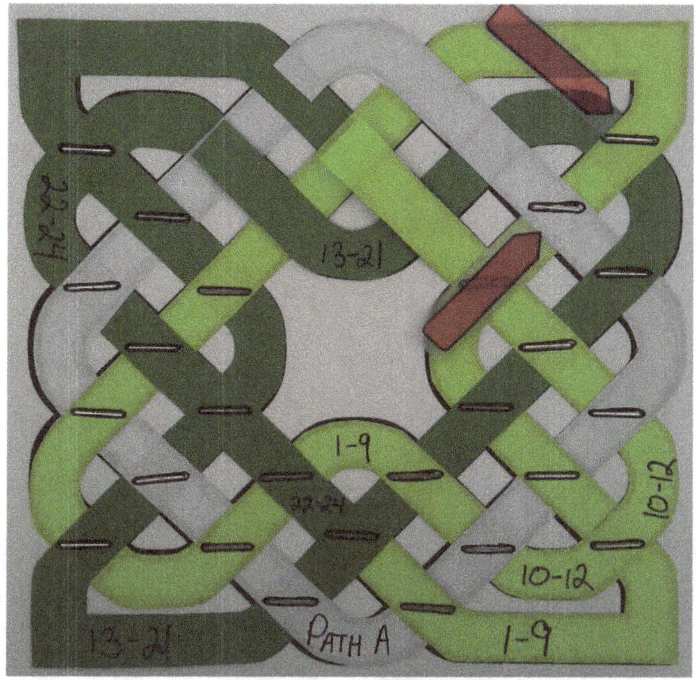

12. Lift right ends of Sections 10-12, 13-21, and Path A out of the way. Lay down Path A, tucking the end under Section 13-21; then Section 13-21, tucking the end under Path A; and then Section 10-12, tucking the end under Section 1-9. Fasten path intersections where indicated.

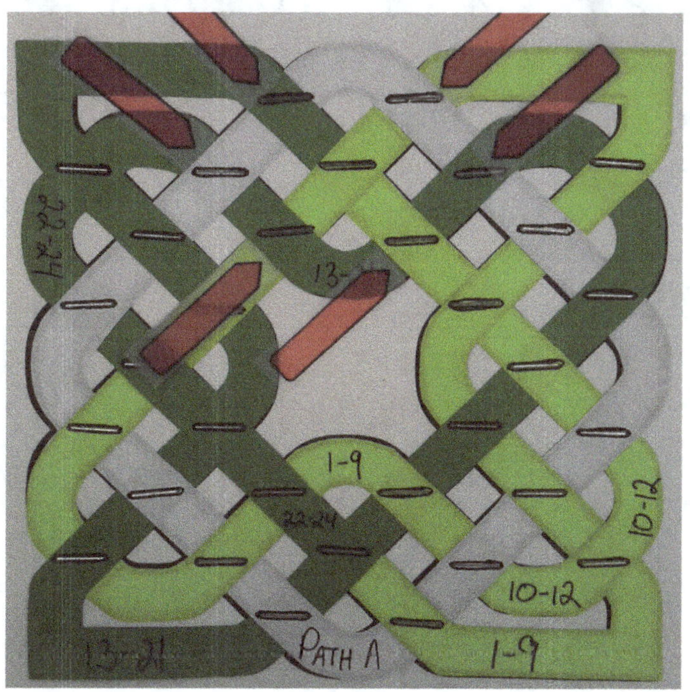

Celtic Knot #3

For the third knot, I divided Path B into thirds and revealed the shape of a heart. I divided the heart so the section wouldn't cross itself. I divided the background in half.

Trace the outline of Path A.
Trace Path B, pieces 1 to 8.
Trace Path B, pieces 9 to 16.
Trace Path B, pieces 17 to 20.
Trace Path B, pieces 21 to 24.

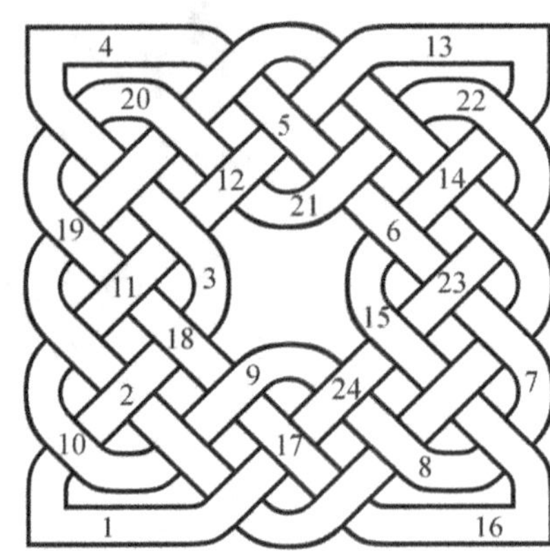

Path A:	Path B:	Path B
Trace Path A	Trace Path B pieces 1-8	Trace Path B pieces 9-16

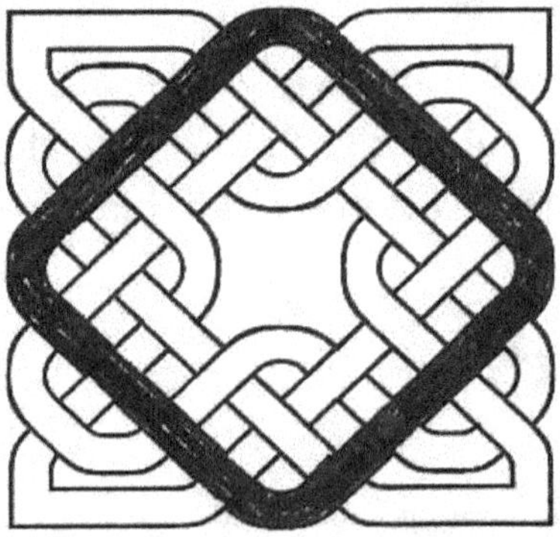

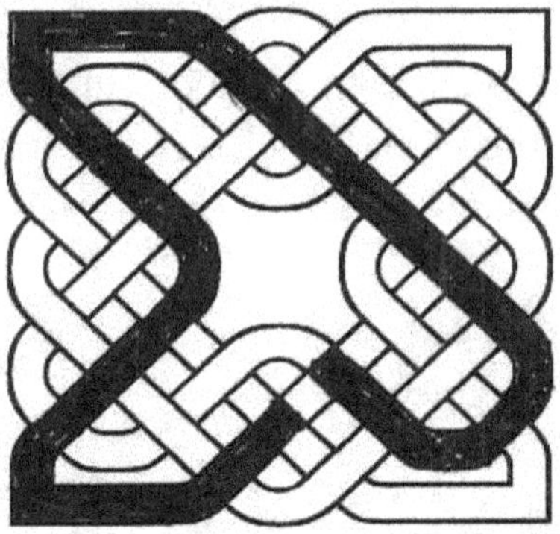

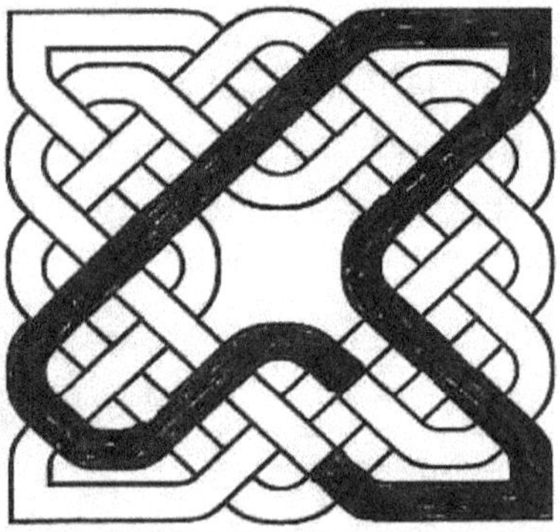

	Path B:	Path B
	Trace Path B pieces 17-20	Trace Path B pieces 21-24

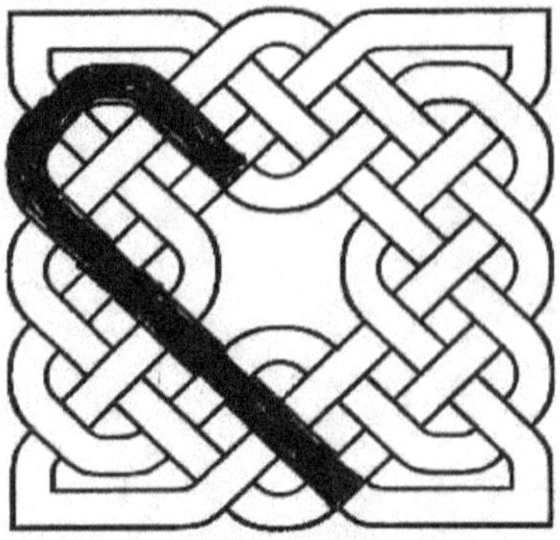

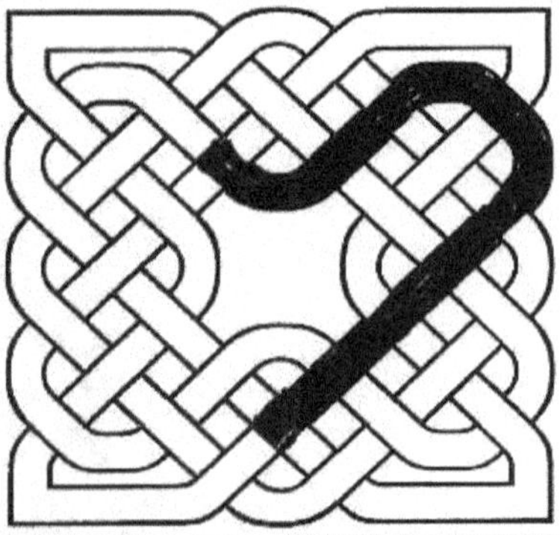

1. Rotate the sections 180 degrees, so the cut ends are at the top of the knot.

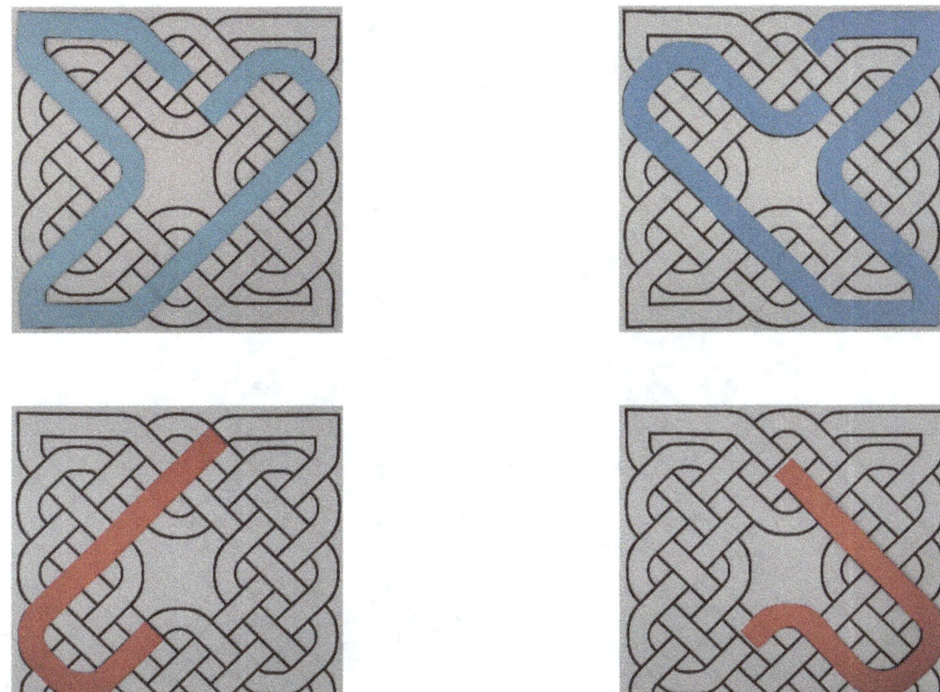

2. Position Section 1-8 on the placement guide; position Path A on top of Section 1-8; position Section 9-16 on top of Path A. Fasten the path intersections to the placement guide along the bottom of the knot to anchor them in place where indicated.

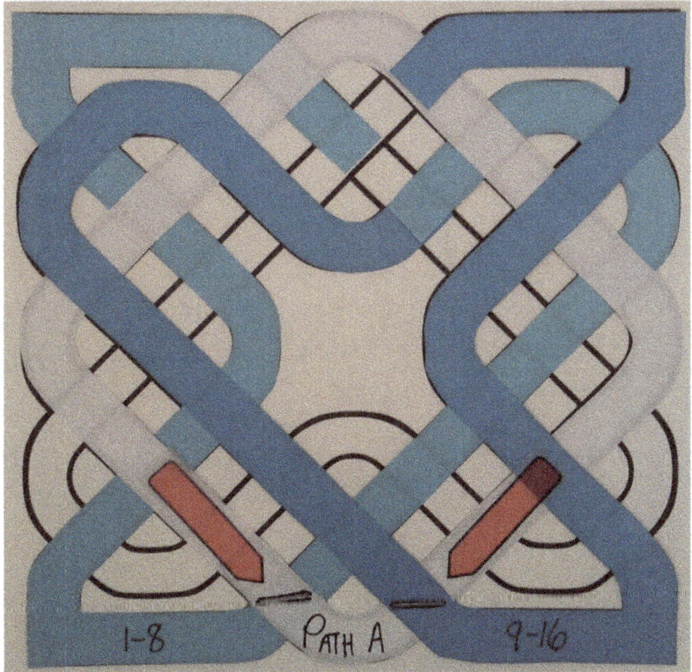

3. At the top of the knot, cut Path A where indicated (the cut ends are tucked under later).

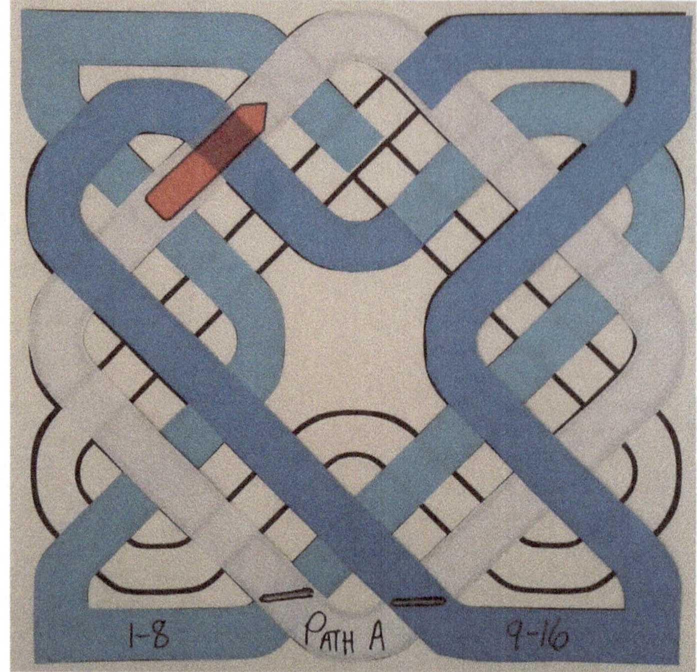

4. Lift left end of Section 9-16 and right end of Section 1-8 out of the way. Lay down Section 9-16, and then Section 1-8. Fasten path intersection where indicated.

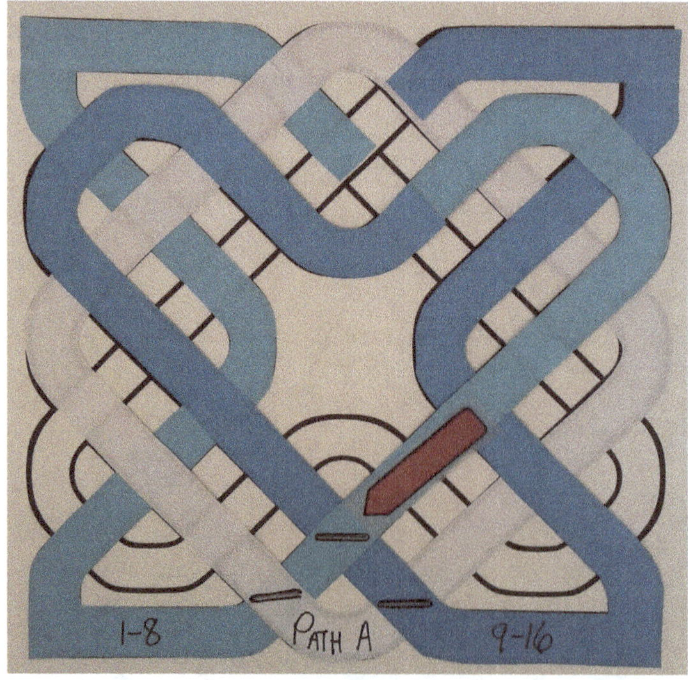

5. Lift right end of Path A out of the way. Position Section 21-24 on the placement guide, tucking left end under Section 9-16. Lay down Path A. Fasten path intersections where indicated.

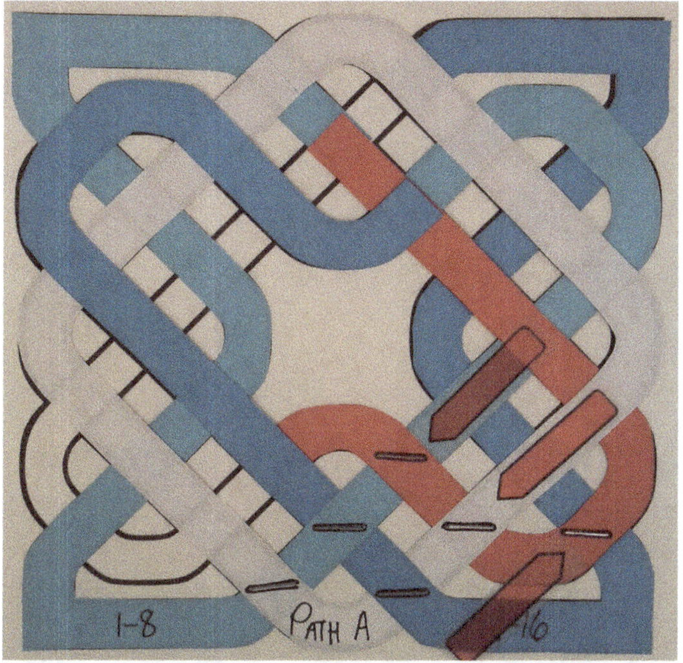

6. Lift right ends of Sections 1-8, 9-16, and Path A out of the way. Lay down Path A, then Section 9-16, and then Section 1-8. Fasten path intersections where indicated.

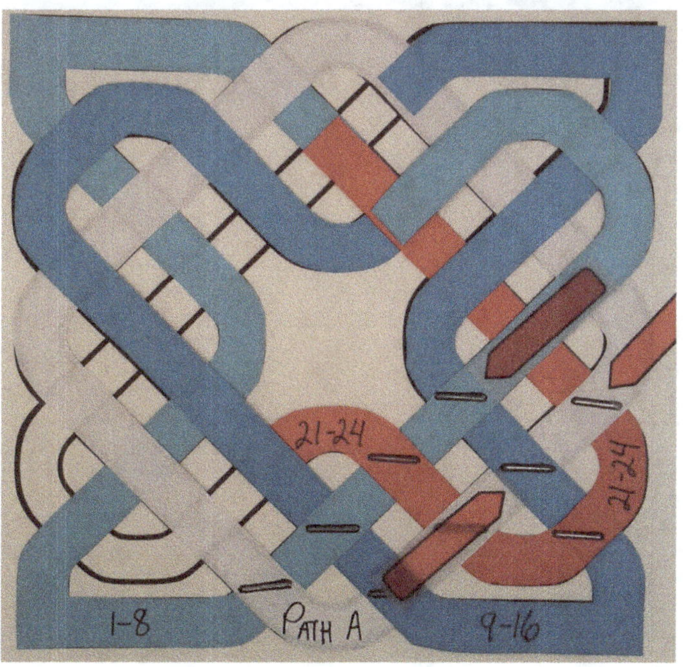

7. Lift right ends of Sections 1-8, 9-16, and 21-24 out of the way. Lay down Section 1-8, then Section 21-24, and then Section 9-16. Fasten path intersections where indicated.

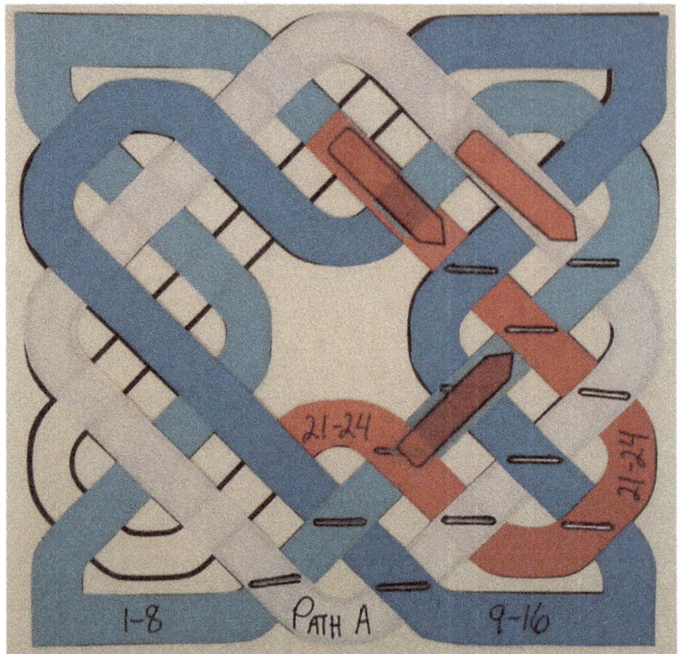

8. Lift right ends of Sections 9-16 and Path A out of the way. Lay down Section 9-16, and then Path A. Fasten path intersections where indicated.

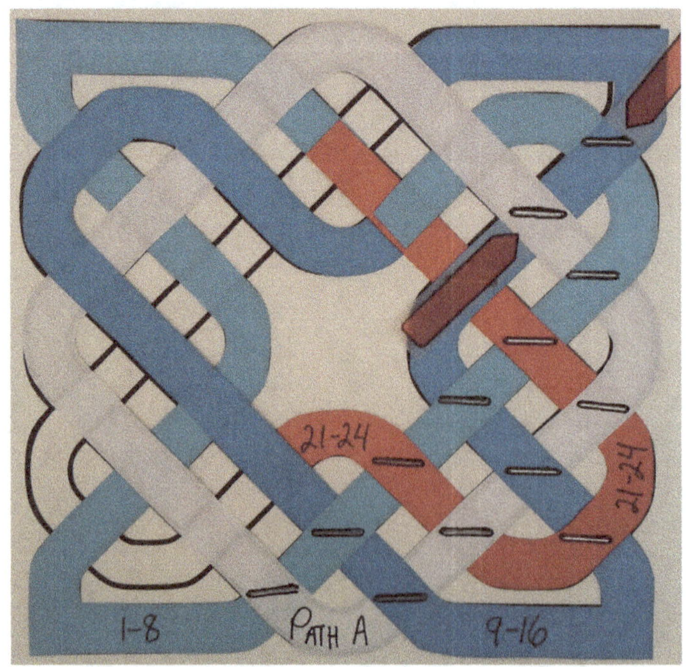

9. Lift right ends of Sections 1-8 and Path A out of the way. Lay down Path A, and then Section 1-8, tucking end under Section 21-24. Fasten path intersection where indicated.

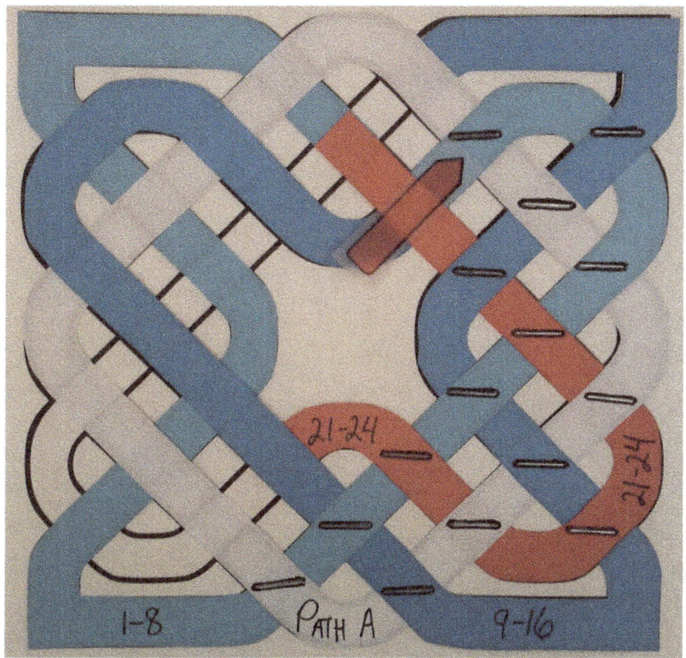

10. Lift left ends of Sections 1-8 and 9-16 out of the way. Position Section 17-20 on the placement guide. Lay down Section 9-16, then lay down Section 1-8. Fasten path intersections where indicated.

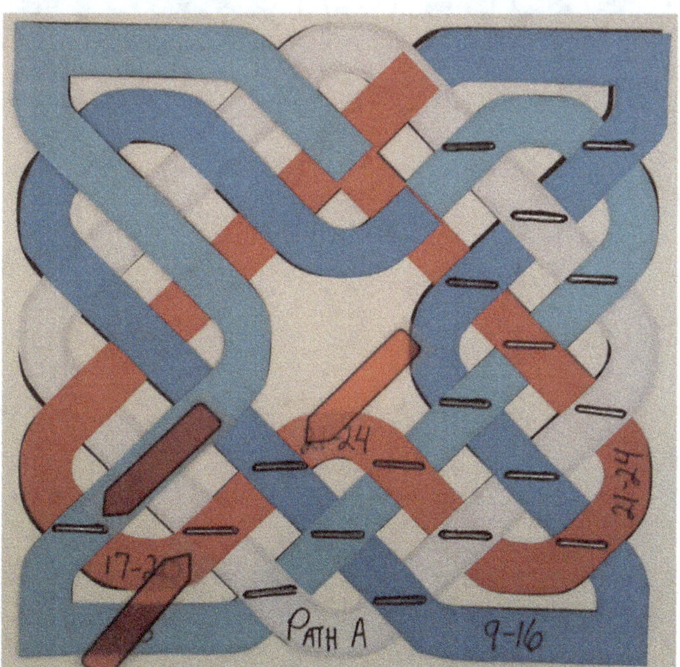

11. Lift left ends of Sections 1-8, 17-20, and Path A out of the way. Lay down Section 1-8, then Path A, and then Section 17-20. Fasten path intersections where indicated.

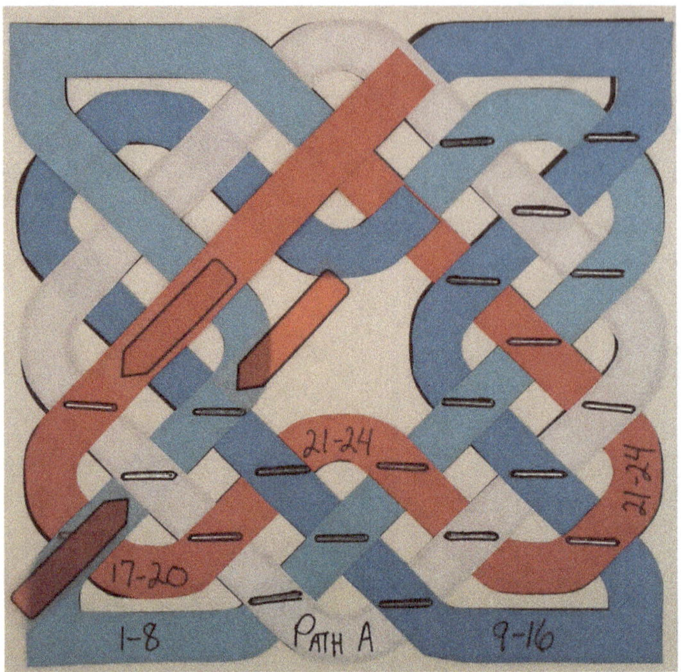

12. Lift left ends of Sections 9-16, 17-20, and Path A out of the way. Lay down Section 17-20, then Section 9-16, and then Path A. Fasten path intersections where indicated.

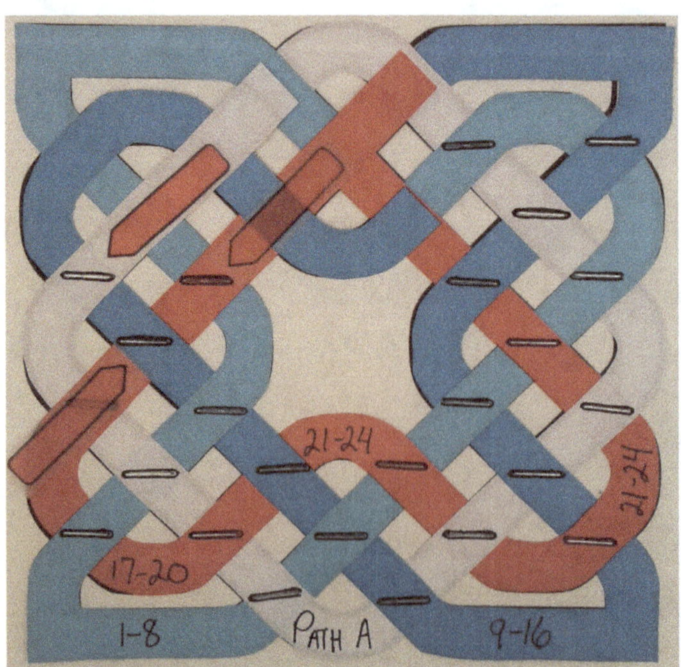

13. Lift left ends of Sections 1-8, 9-16, and Path A out of the way. Lay down Path A, then Section 1-8, and then Section 9-16. Fasten path intersections where indicated.

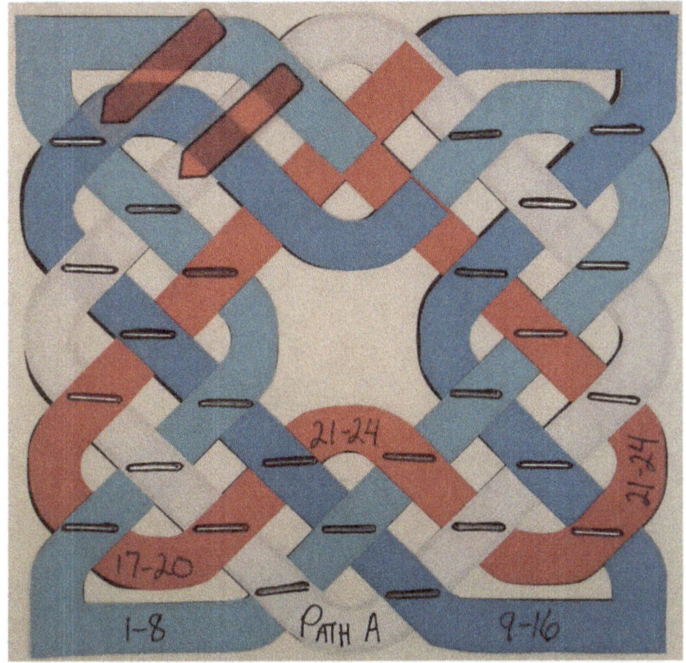

14. Lift left ends of Sections 1-8, 9-16, and Path A out of the way. Lay down Section 9-16, tucking end under Section 21-24; lay down Path A, tucking end under Section 1-8; lay down Section 1-8, tucking end under Section 17-20. Tuck end of Section 17-20 under Path A. Fasten path intersections where indicated.

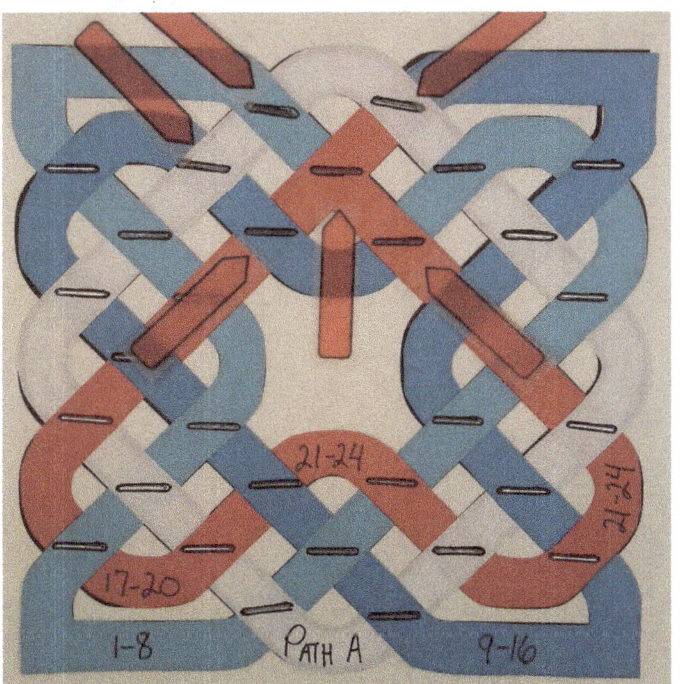

15. Rotate the knot to reveal the heart.

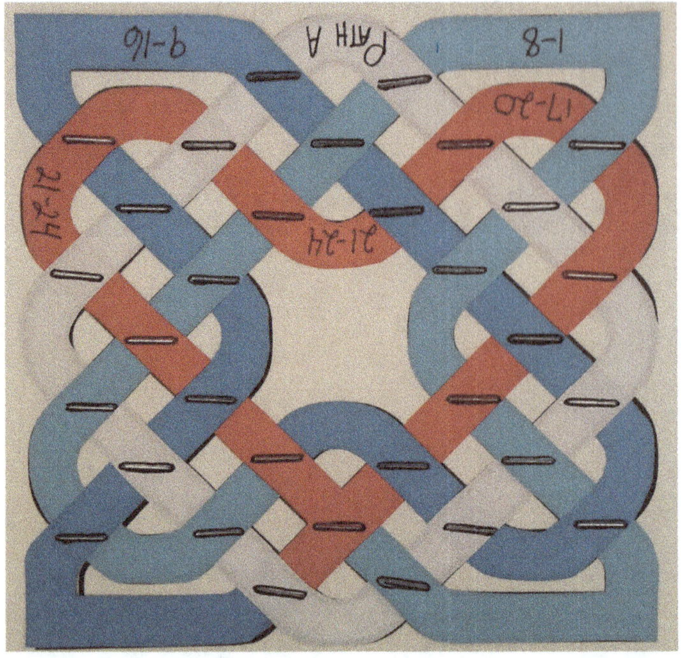

Celtic Knot #4

For the fourth knot, I divided Path B into thirds and revealed the shape of a heart. I divided the heart so the section wouldn't cross itself. I divided the background into thirds.

Trace the outline of Path A.
Trace Path B, pieces 1 to 5.
Trace Path B, pieces 6 to 11.
Trace Path B, pieces 12 to 16.
Trace Path B, pieces 17 to 20.
Trace Path B, pieces 21 to 24.

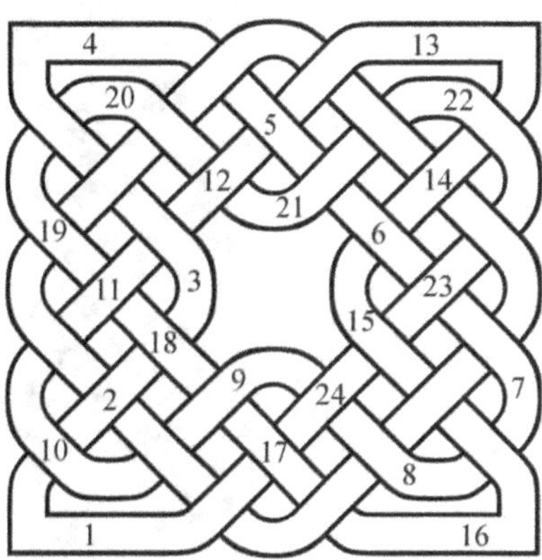

Path A:	Path B:	Path B
Trace Path A	Trace Path B pieces 1-5	Trace Path B pieces 6-11

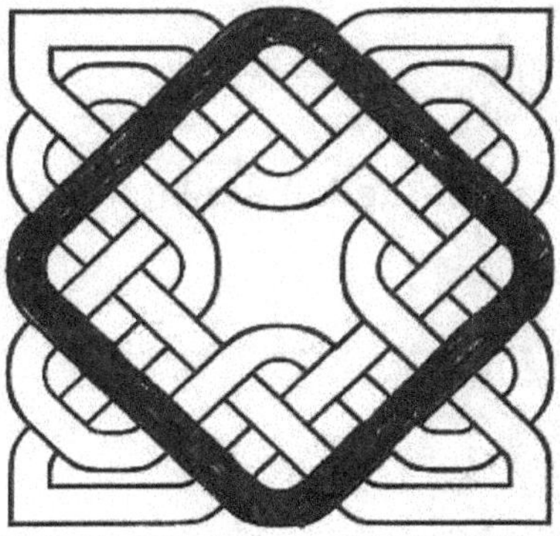

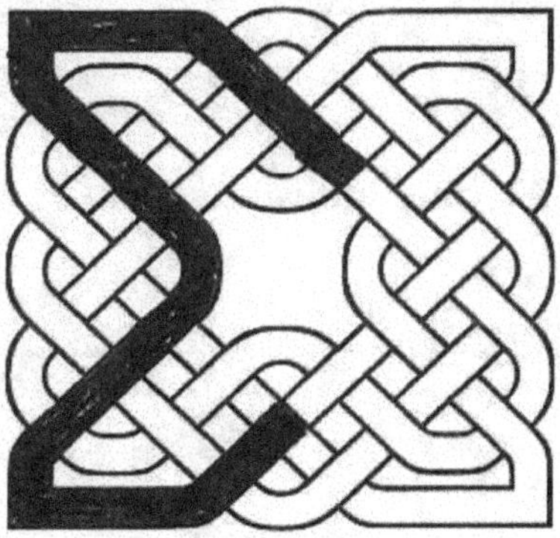

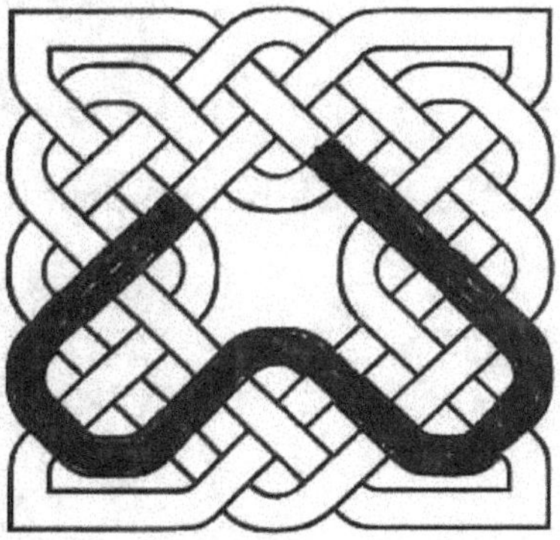

Path B:	Path B:	Path B
Trace Path B pieces 12-16	Trace Path B pieces 17-20	Trace Path B pieces 21-24

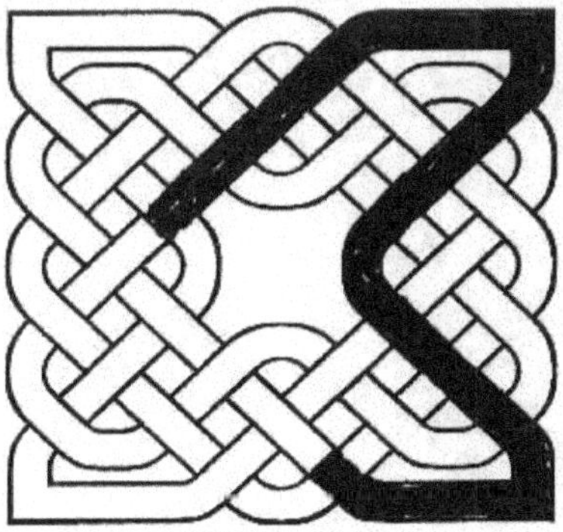

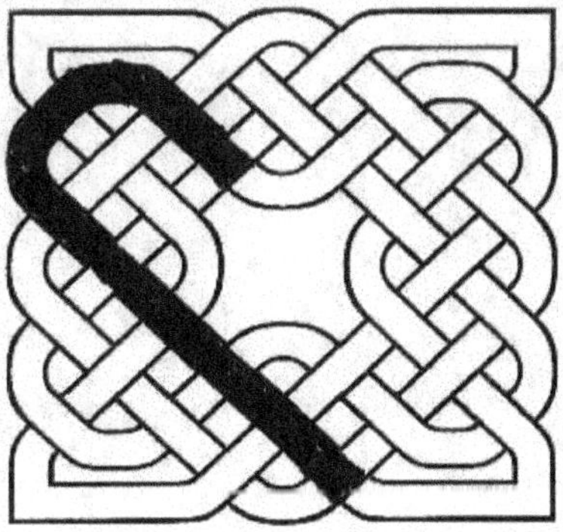

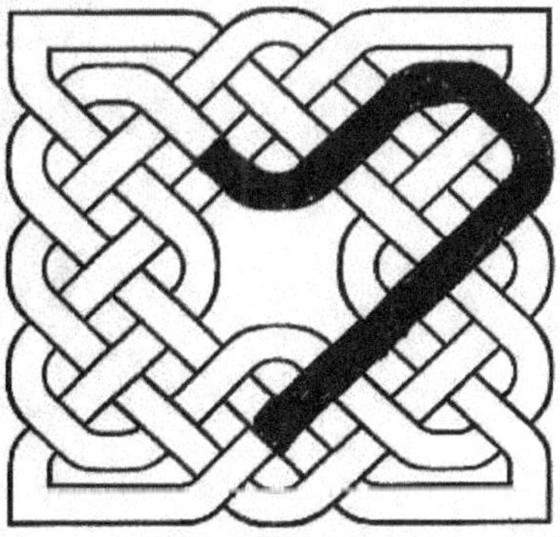

1. Position Section 12-16 on the placement guide; position Section 17-20 on the placement guide; position Path A on top of the juncture of Sections 12-16 and 17-20; position Section 1-5 on top of Path A. Fasten the path intersections to the placement guide along the bottom of the knot to anchor them in place where indicated.

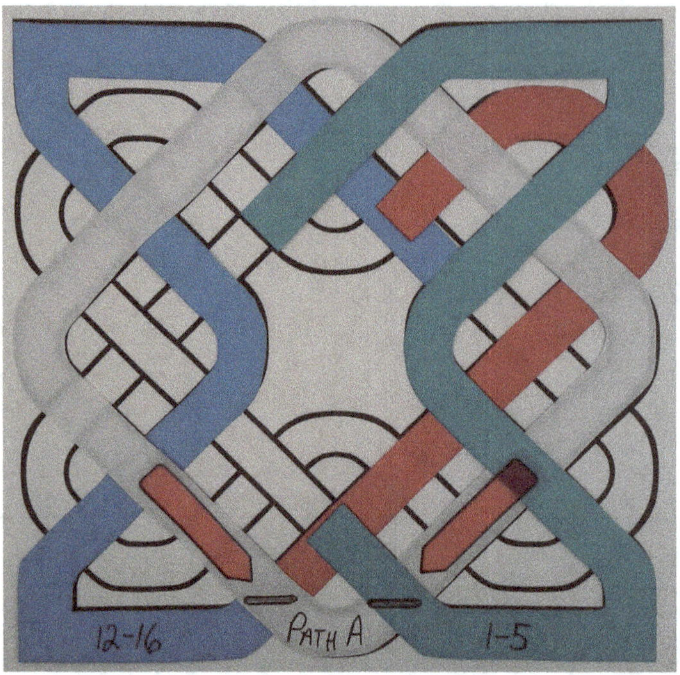

2. At the top of the knot, cut Path A where indicated (the cut ends are tucked under later).

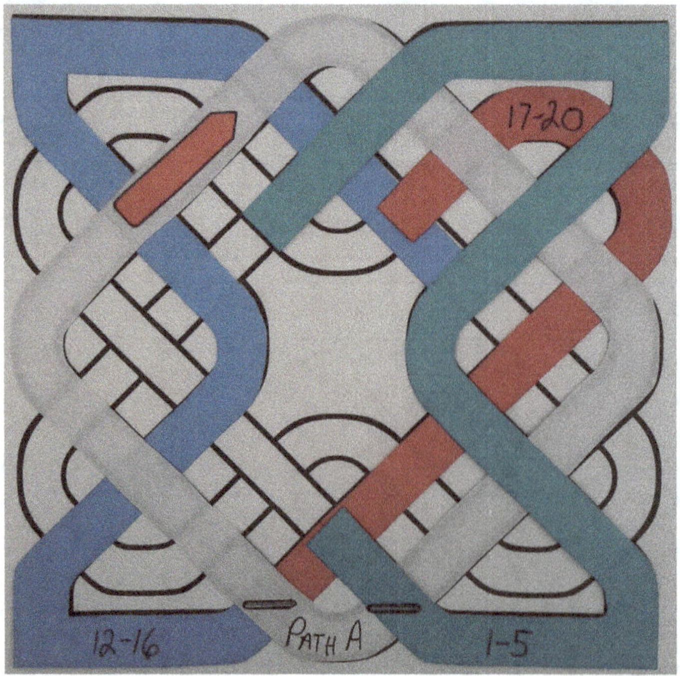

3. Lift Section 17-20 out of the way. Position Section 21-24 on the placement guide. Lay down Section 17-20. Fasten path intersection where indicated.

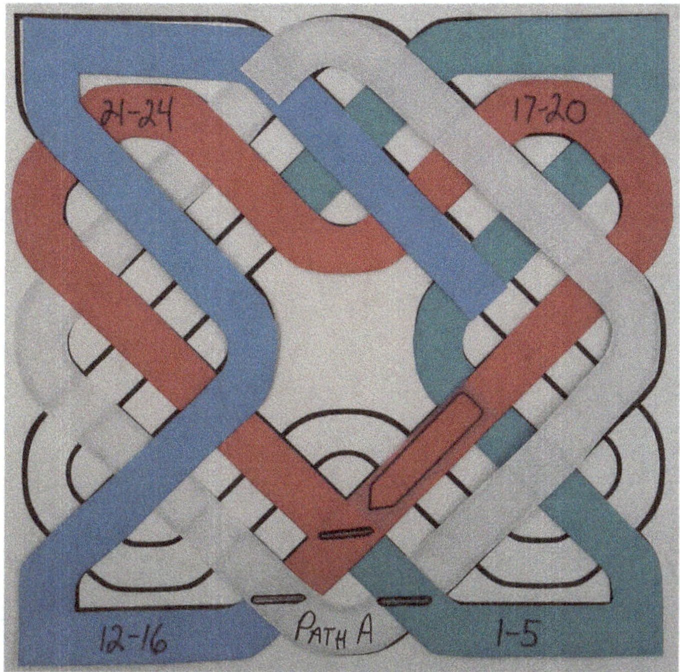

4. Lift Sections 12-16, 21-24, and the right end of Path A out of the way. Position Section 6-11 on the placement guide. Lay down Sections 12-16, 21-24, and the right end of Path A. Fasten path intersections where indicated.

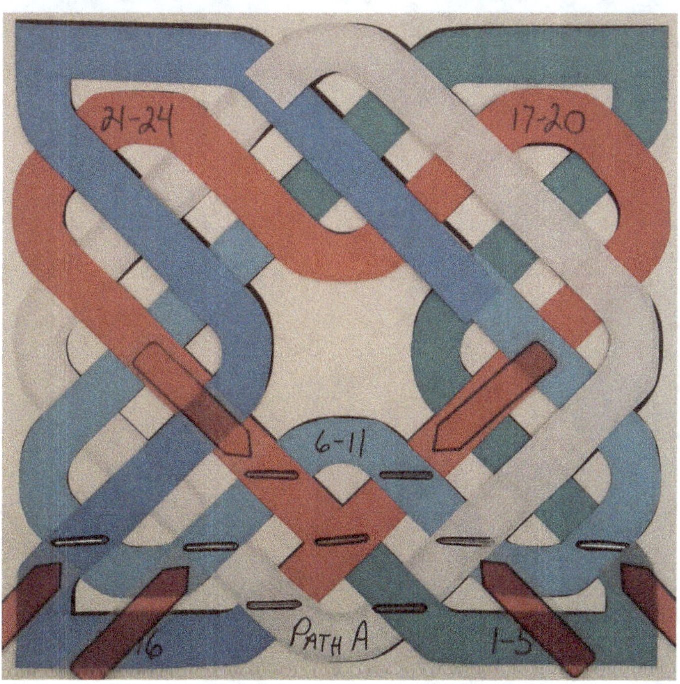

5. Lift left ends of Sections 6-11, 12-16, and Path A out of the way. Lay down Section 12-16, then Path A, and then Section 6-11. Fasten path intersections where indicated.

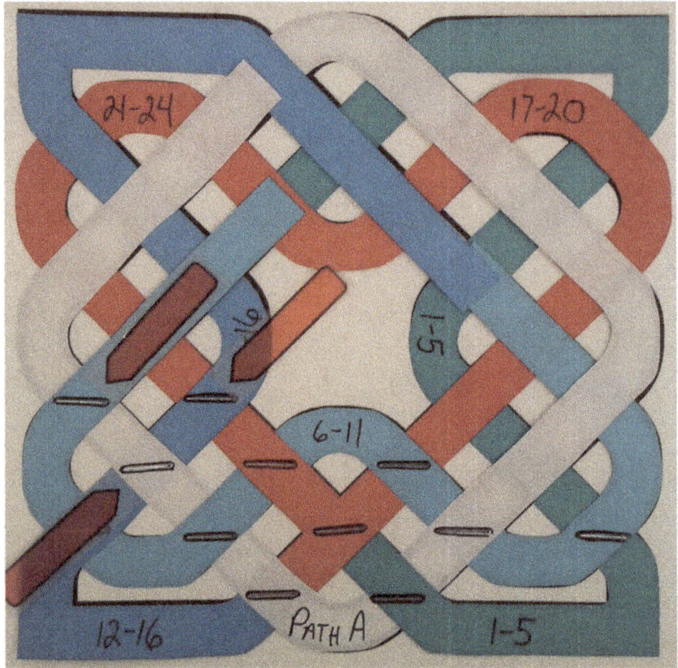

6. Lift left ends of Sections 6-11, 21-24, and Path A out of the way. Lay down Section 6-11, then Section 21-24, and then Path A. Fasten path intersections where indicated.

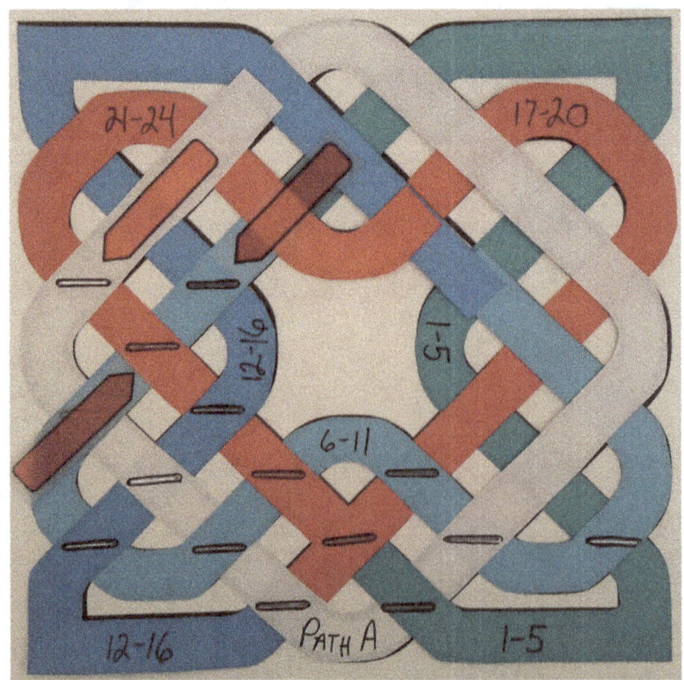

7. Lift Sections 12-16, 21-24, and Path A out of the way. Lay down Path A, then Section 12-16, and then Section 21-24. Fasten path intersections where indicated.

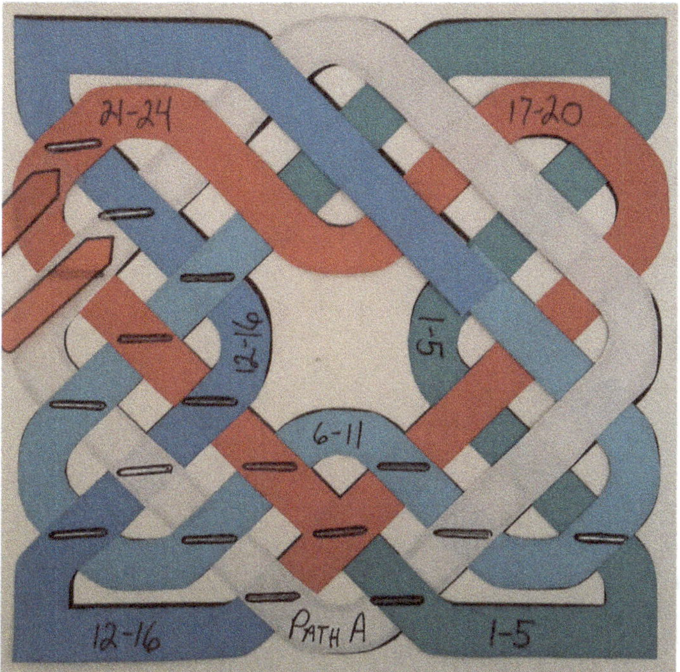

8. Lift Section 21-24, and Path A out of the way. Lay down Section 21-24, then Path A, tucking end under Section 12-16. Fasten path intersection where indicated.

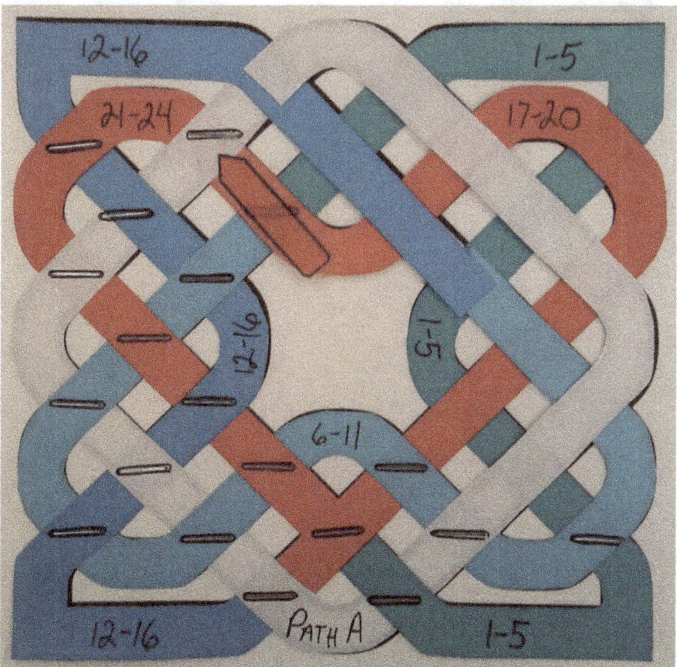

9. Lift Sections 1-5, 17-20, and Path A out of the way. Lay down Path A, then Section 1-5, and then Section 17-20. Fasten path intersections where indicated.

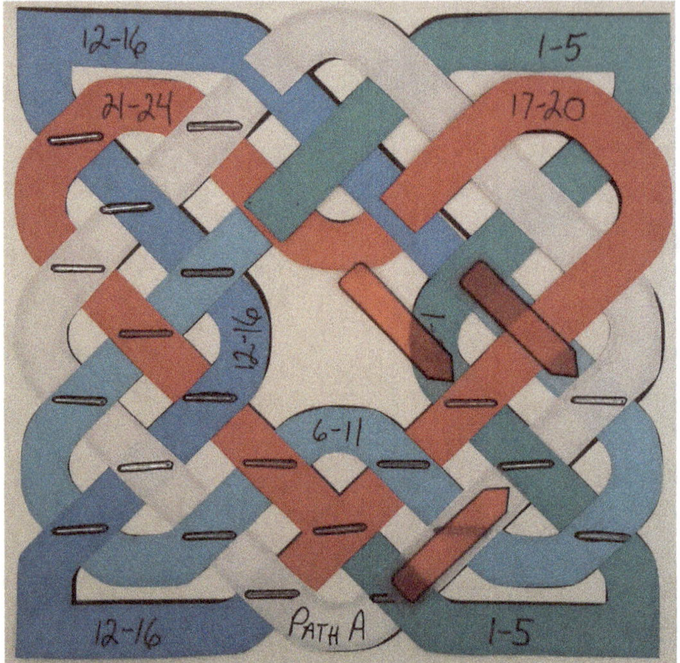

10. Lift Sections 1-5, 6-11, and 17-20 out of the way. Lay down Section 17-20, then Section 6-11, and then Section 1-5. Fasten path intersections where indicated.

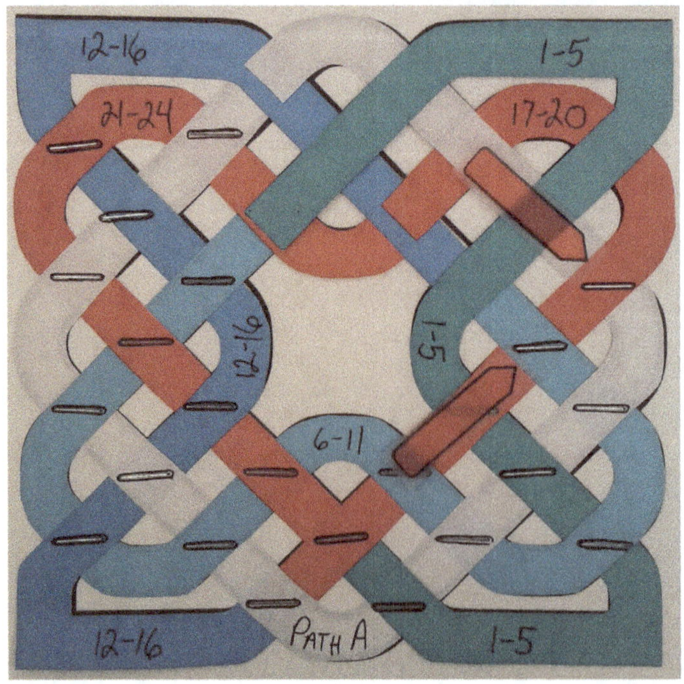

11. Lift Section 1-5 and Path A out of the way. Lay down Section 1-5, and then Path A. Fasten path intersections where indicated.

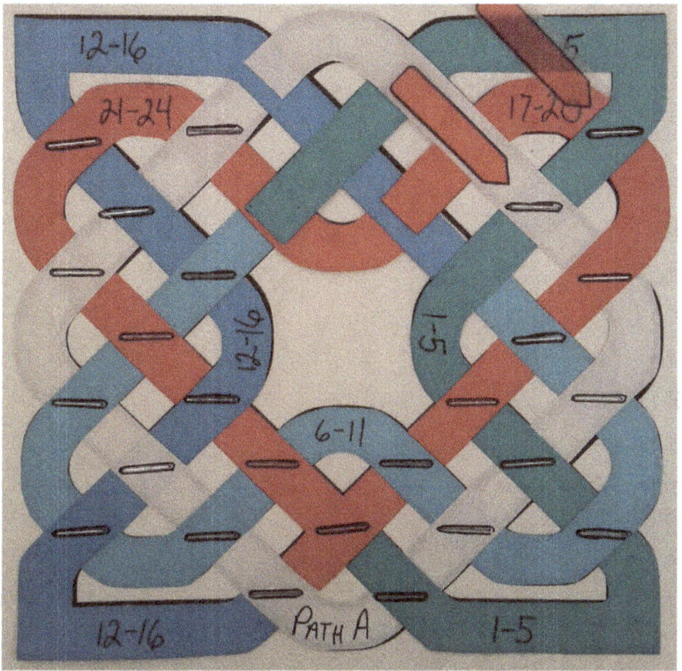

12. Lift Section 17-20 and Path A out of the way. Lay down Path A, tucking end under Section 12-16; lay down Section 17-20, tucking end under Section 12-16. Tuck end of Section 1-5 under Section 21-24. Fasten path intersections where indicated.

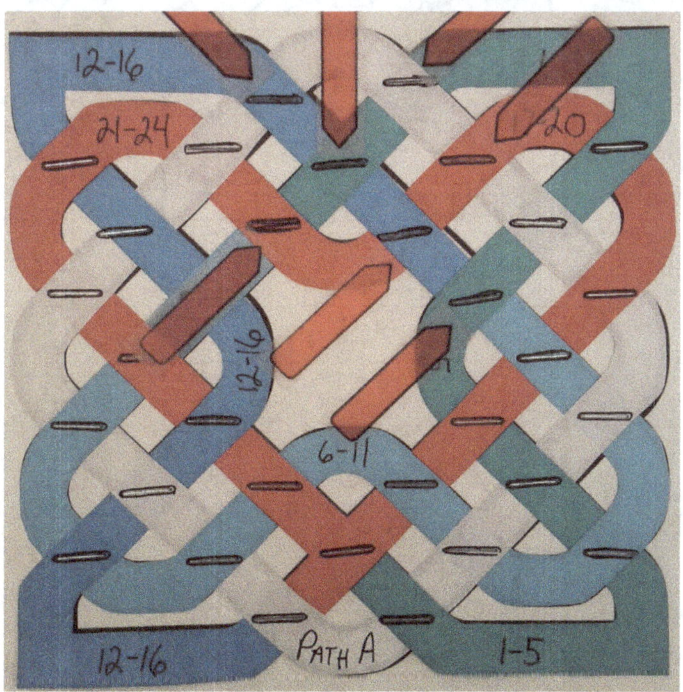

Celtic Knot #5

For the fifth knot, I first divided Path B into thirds and revealed the shape of a heart. Next, I divided the heart so the section wouldn't cross itself. Then, I divided the background into fourths. This is the same as dividing Path B into sixths.

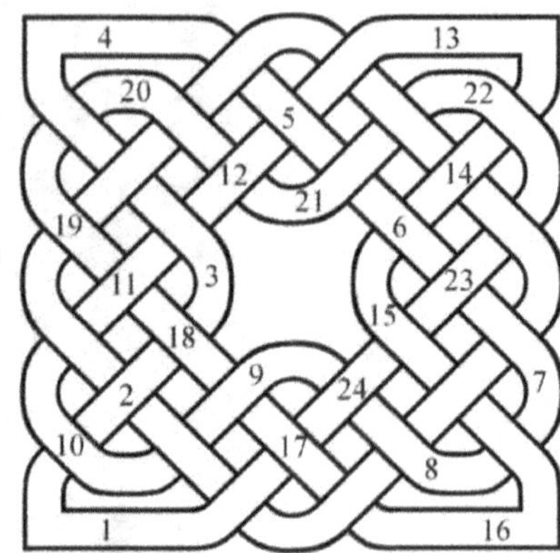

Trace the outline of Path A.
Trace Path B, pieces 1 to 4.
Trace Path B, pieces 5 to 8.
Trace Path B, pieces 9 to 12.
Trace Path B, pieces 13 to 16.
Trace Path B, pieces 17 to 20.
Trace Path B, pieces 21 to 24.

Path A:	Path B:	Path B
Trace Path A	Trace Path B pieces 1-4	Trace Path B pieces 5-8

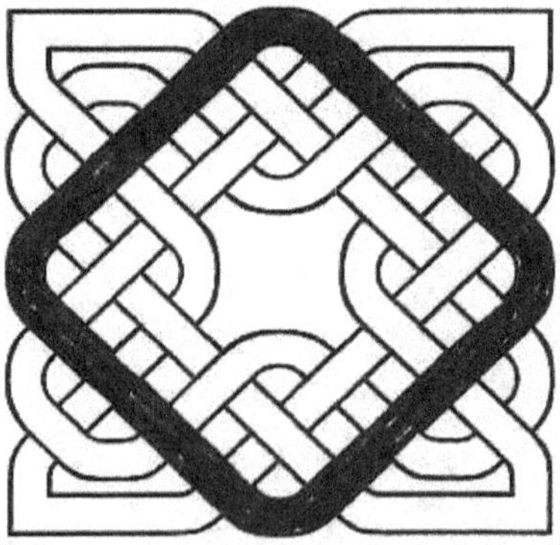

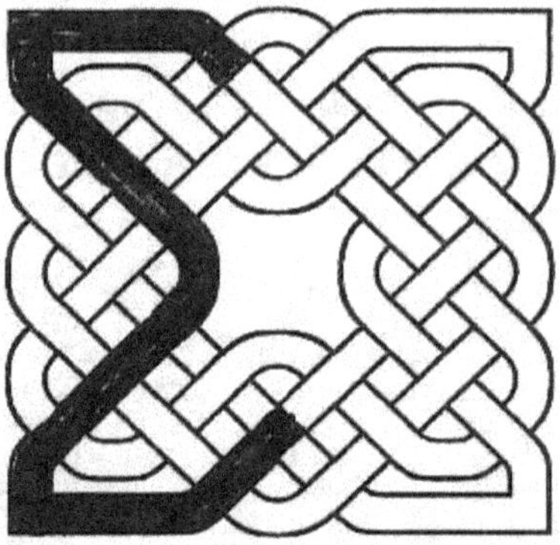

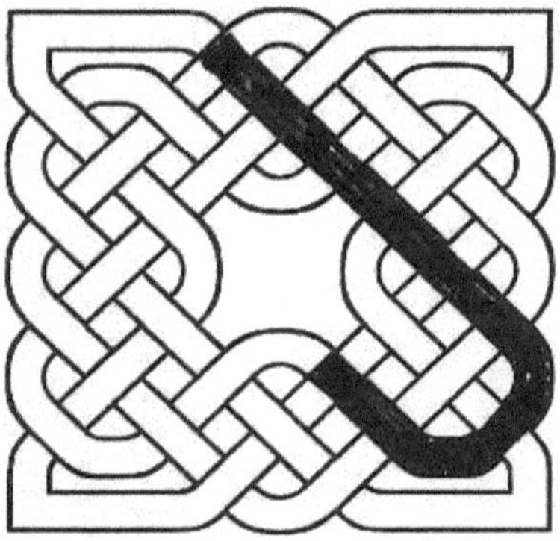

	Path B:	Path B
	Trace Path B pieces 9-12	Trace Path B pieces 13-16

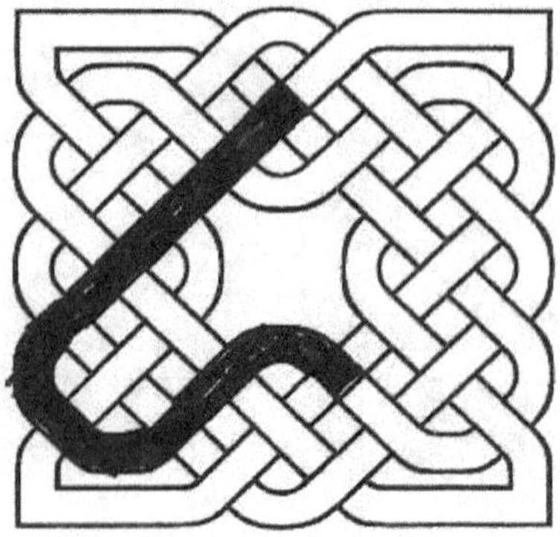

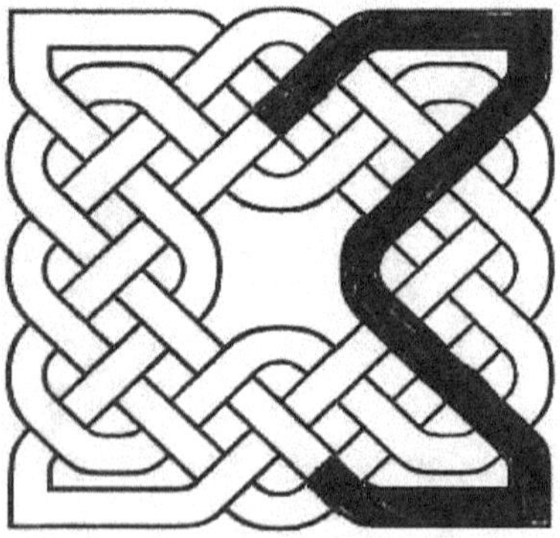

	Path B:	Path B
	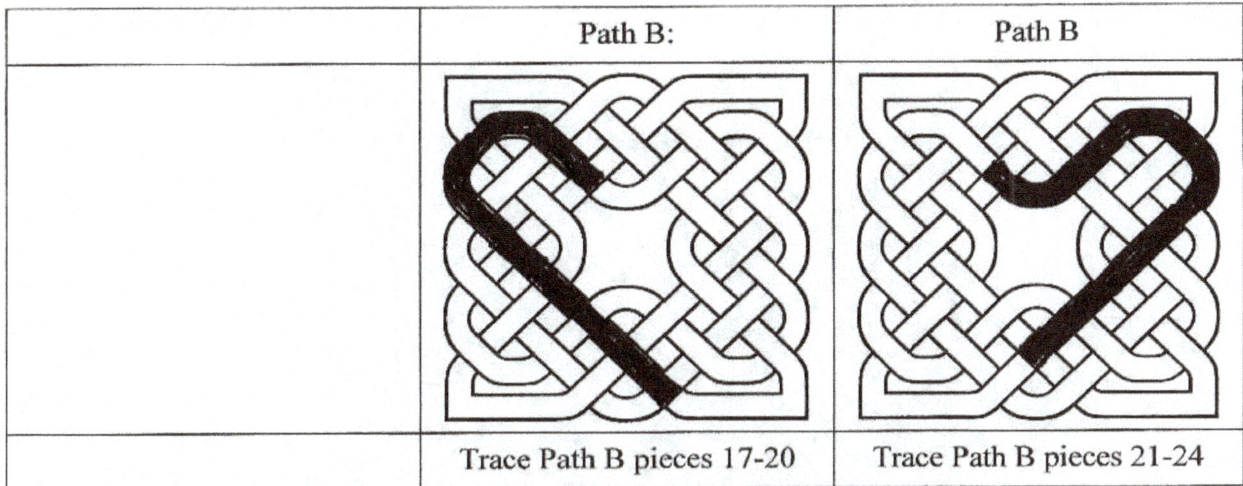	
	Trace Path B pieces 17-20	Trace Path B pieces 21-24

1. Position Section 13-16 on the placement guide; position Section 17-20 on the placement guide; position Path A on top of the juncture of Sections 13-16 and 17-20; position Section 1-4 on top of Path A. Fasten the path intersections to the placement guide along the bottom of the knot to anchor them in place where indicated.

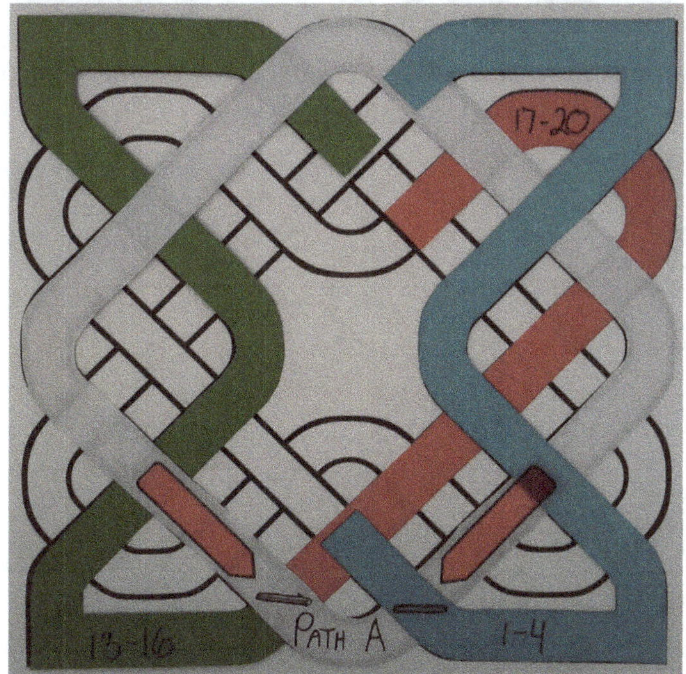

2. At the top of the knot, cut Path A where indicated (the cut ends are tucked under later).

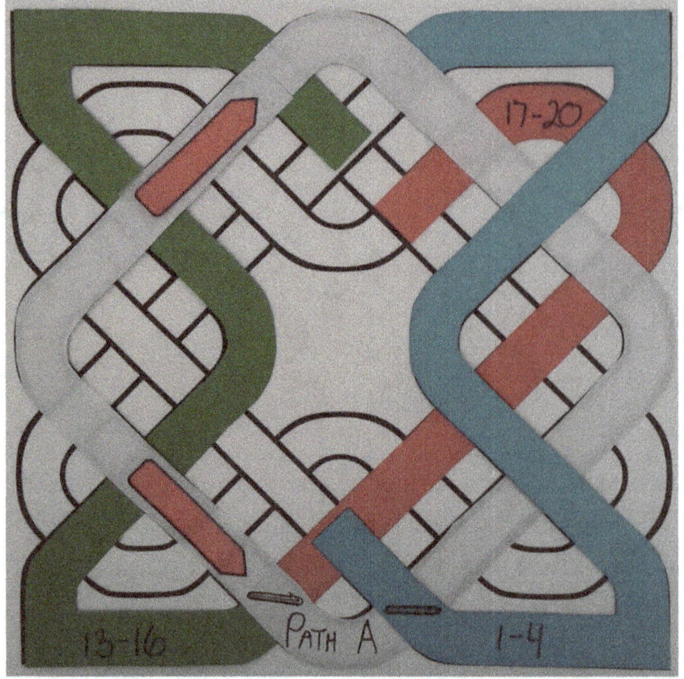

3. Lift Section 17-20 out of the way. Position Section 21-24 on the placement guide. Lay down Section 17-20. Fasten path intersection where indicated.

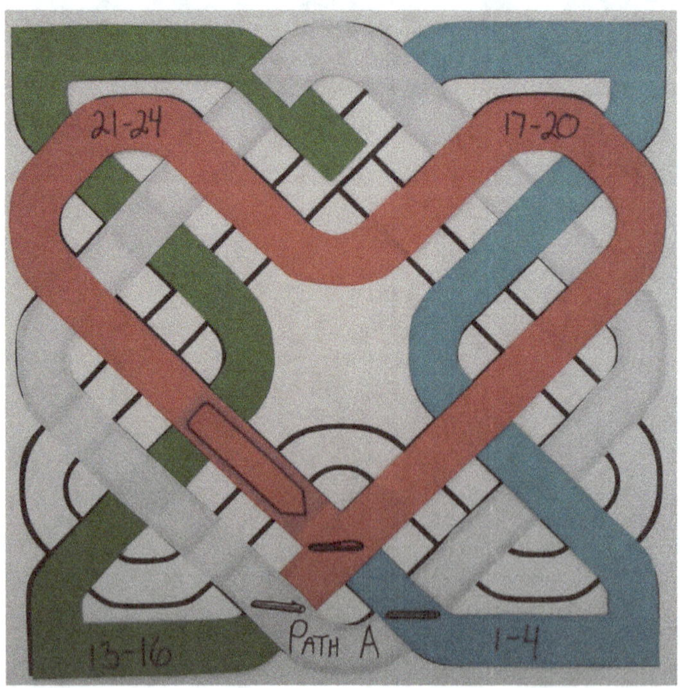

46

4. Lift Sections 13-16 and 21-24 out of the way. Position Section 5-8 on the placement guide. Lay down Sections 13-16 and 21-24. Fasten path intersections where indicated.

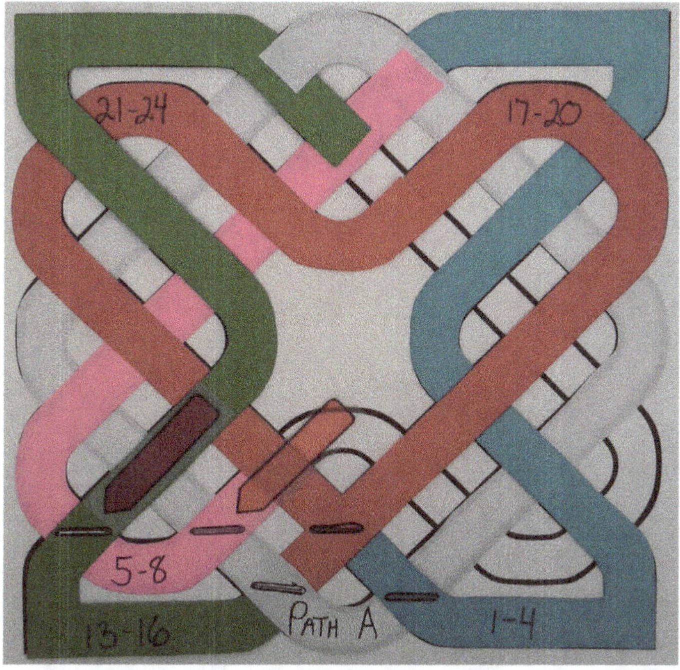

5. Lift the right end of Path A and Section 21-24 out of the way. Position Section 9-12 on the placement guide. Lay down Section 21-24 and Path A. Fasten path intersections where indicated.

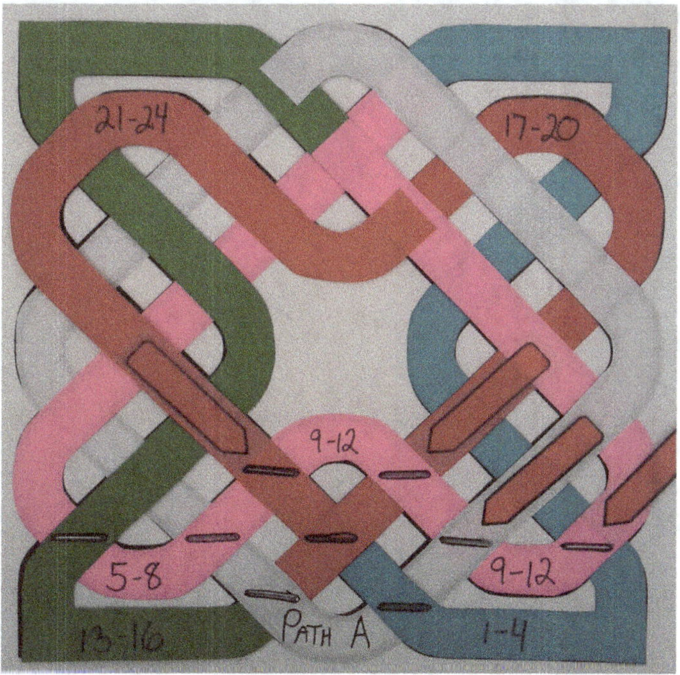

6. Lift Sections 1-4, 17-20, and Path A out of the way. Lay down Path A, then Section 1-4, and then Section 17-20. Fasten path intersections where indicated.

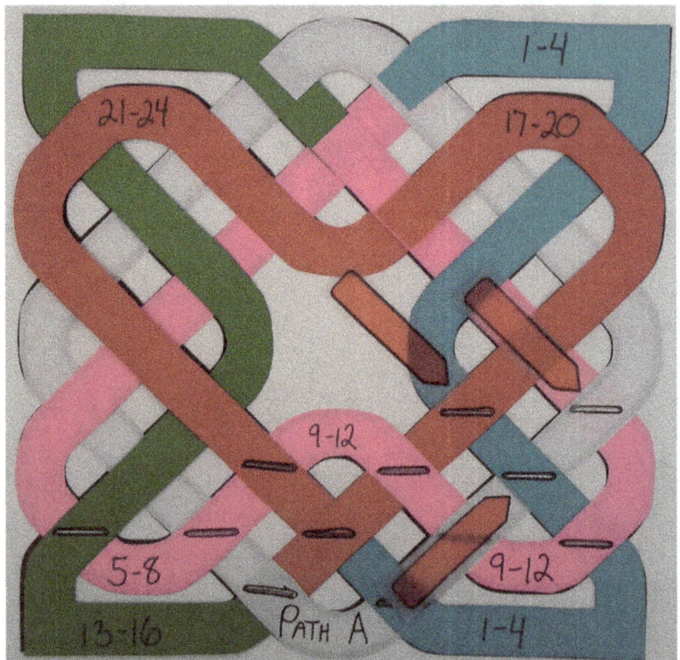

7. Lift Sections 1-4, 9-12, and 17-20 out of the way. Lay down Section 17-20, then Section 9-12, and then Section 1-4. Fasten path intersections where indicated.

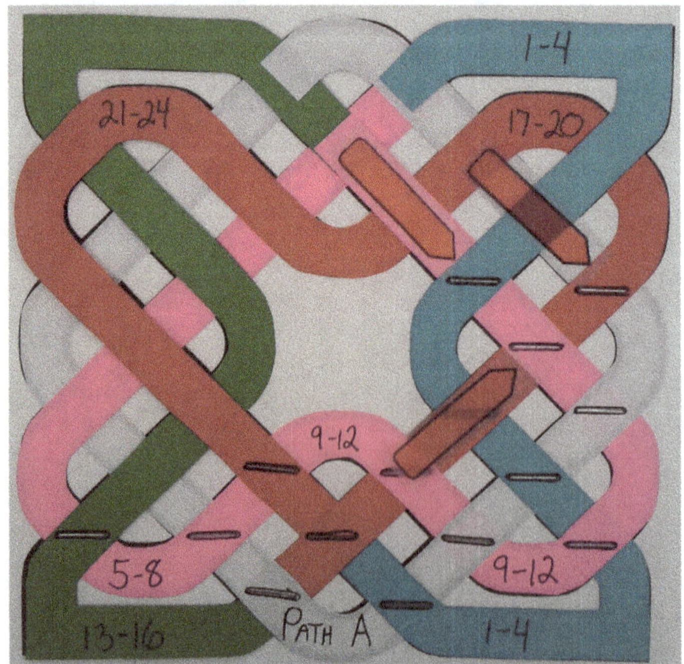

8. Lift Sections 1-4 and Path A out of the way. Lay down Section 1-4, and then Path A. Fasten path intersections where indicated.

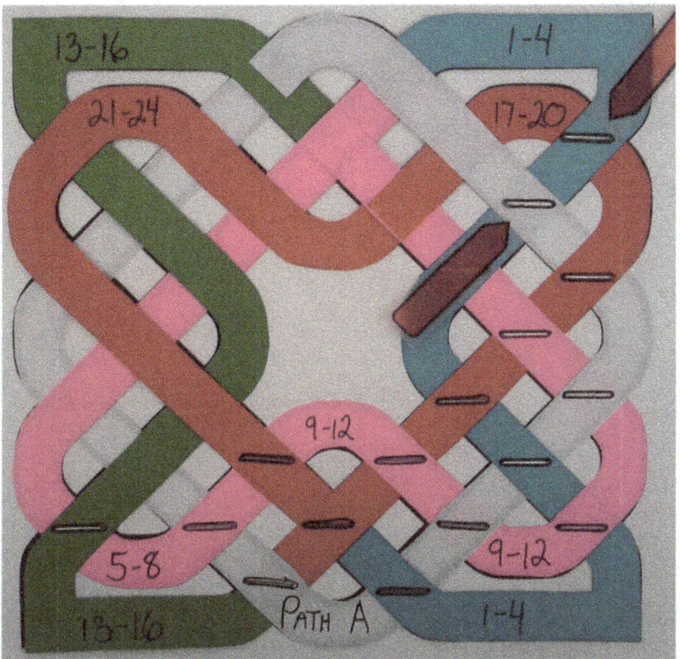

9. Lift Sections 9-12, 17-20, and Path A out of the way. Lay down Path A, tucking end under Section 13-16; lay down Section 17-20; then lay down Section 9-12. Fasten path intersection where indicated.

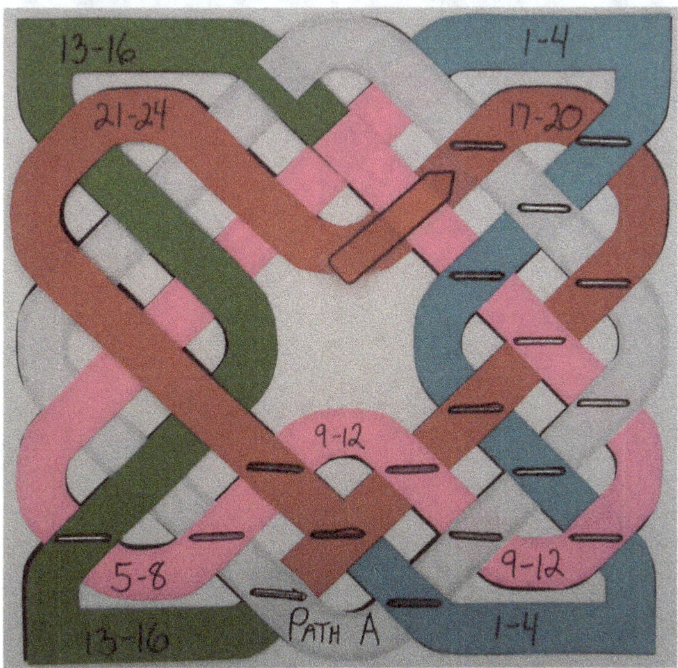

10. Lift Sections 5-8, 13-16, and Path A out of the way. Lay down Section 13-16, then Path A, and then Section 5-8. Fasten path intersections where indicated.

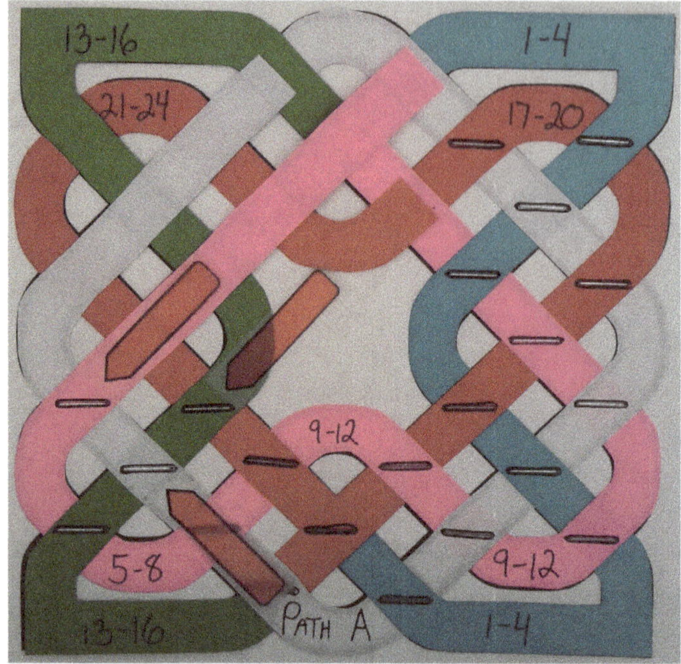

11. Lift Sections 5-8, 21-24, and Path A out of the way. Lay down Section 5-8, then Section 21-24, and then Path A. Fasten path intersections where indicated.

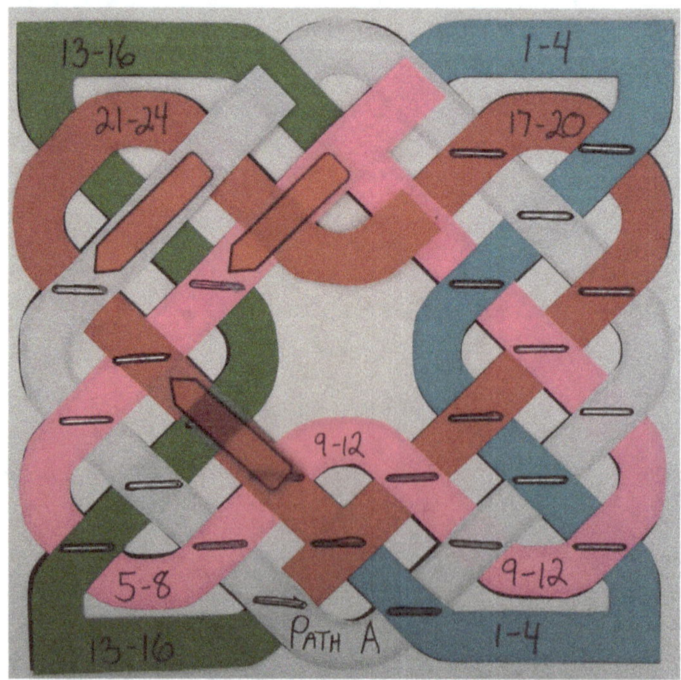

12. Lift Sections 13-16, 21-24, and Path A out of the way. Lay down Path A, then Section 13-16, and then Section 21-24. Fasten path intersections where indicated.

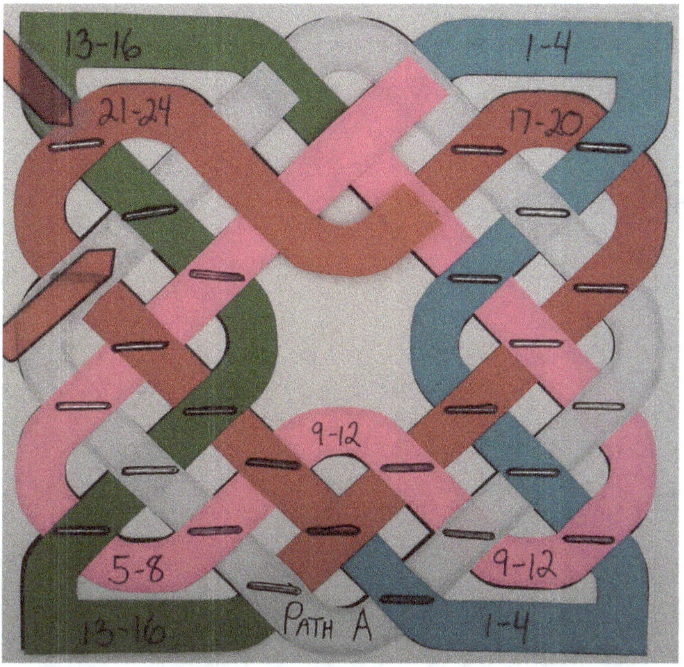

13. Lift sections 21-24 and Path A out of the way. Lay down Section 21-24, tucking end under Section 9-12; then lay down Path A, tucking end under Section 13-16. Tuck end of Section 5-8 under Path A. Fasten path intersections where indicated.

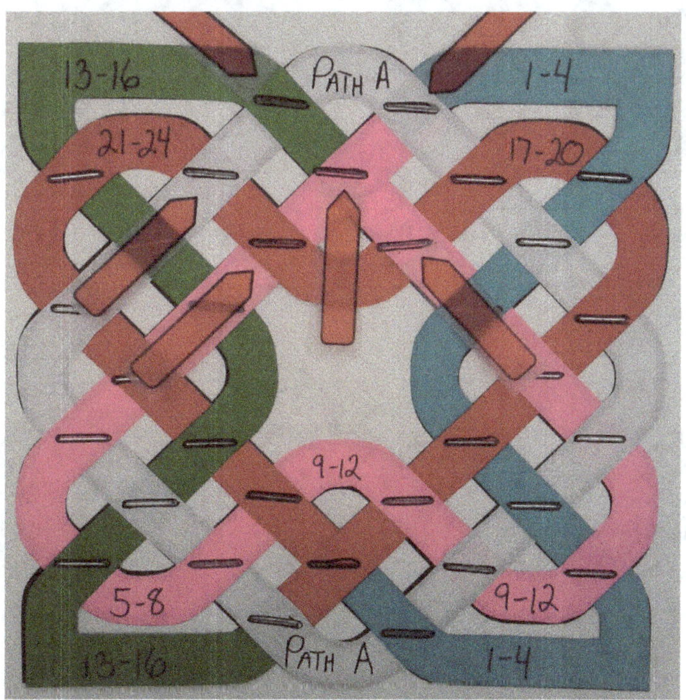

Celtic Knot #6

For this knot, I divided Path B into thirds and revealed the shape of a heart. I divided the heart so the section wouldn't cross itself, then I divided the background into fifths (one section has one piece more than the other four).

Trace the outline of Path A
Trace Path B, pieces 1 to 3.
Trace Path B, pieces 4 to 6.
Trace Path B, pieces 7 to 10.
Trace Path B, pieces 11 to 13.
Trace Path B, pieces 14 to 16.
Trace Path B, pieces 17 to 20.
Trace Path B, pieces 21 to 24.

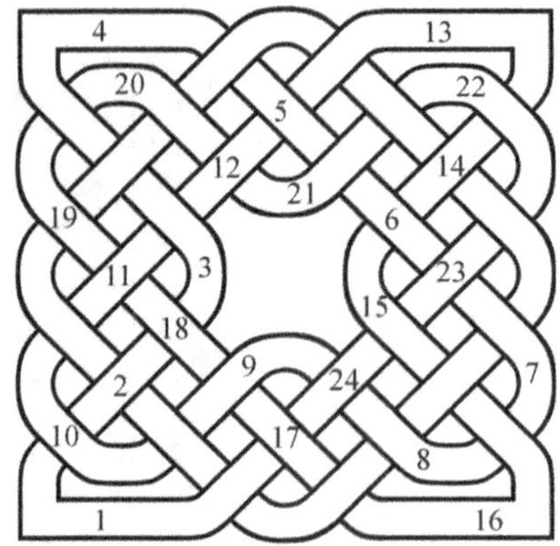

Path A:	Path B:	Path B
Trace Path A	Trace Path B pieces 1-3	Trace Path B pieces 4-6

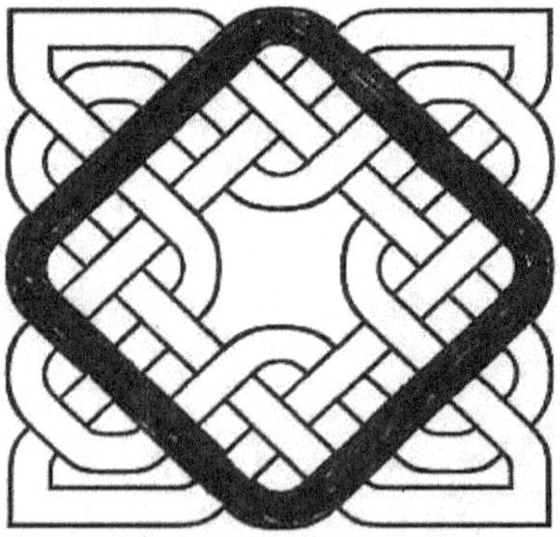

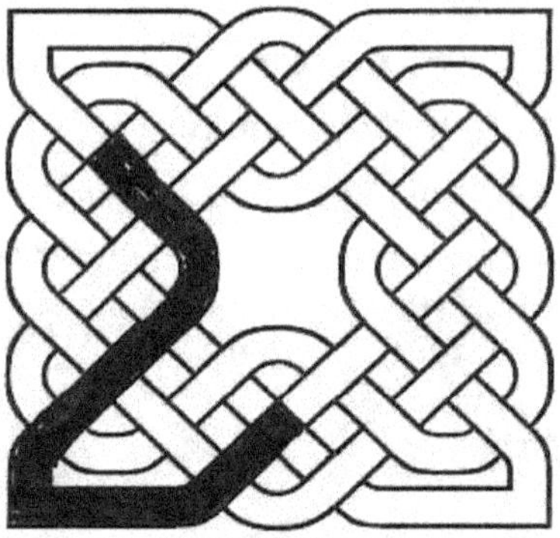

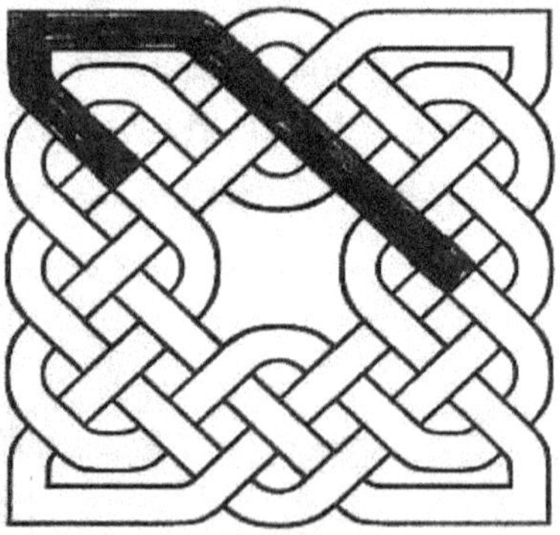

Path B:	Path B:	Path B
Trace Path B pieces 7-10	Trace Path B pieces 11-13	Trace Path B pieces 14-16

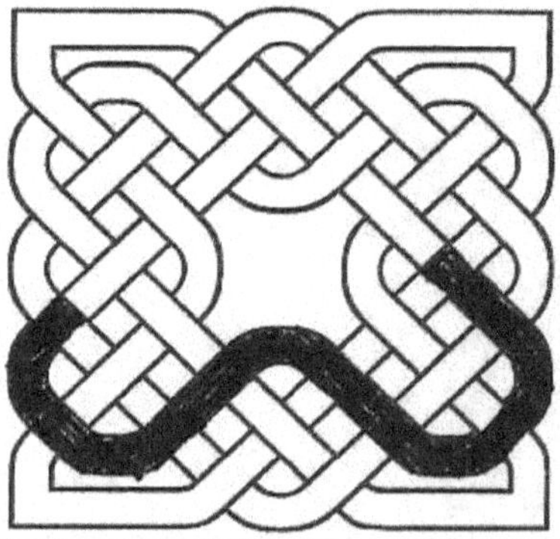

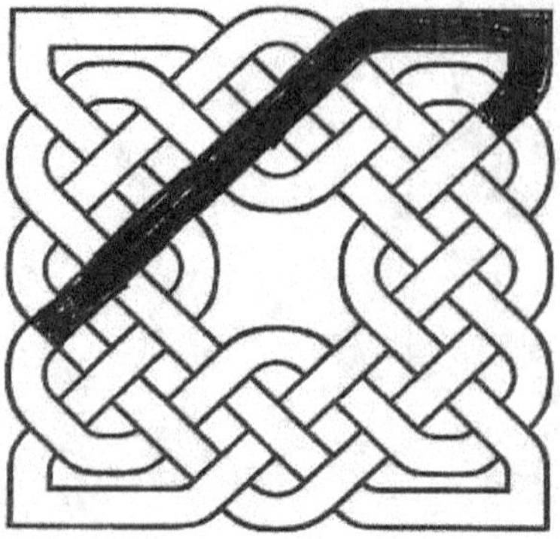

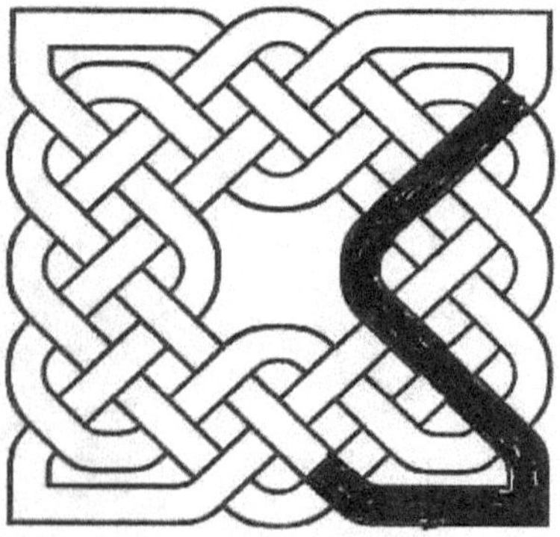

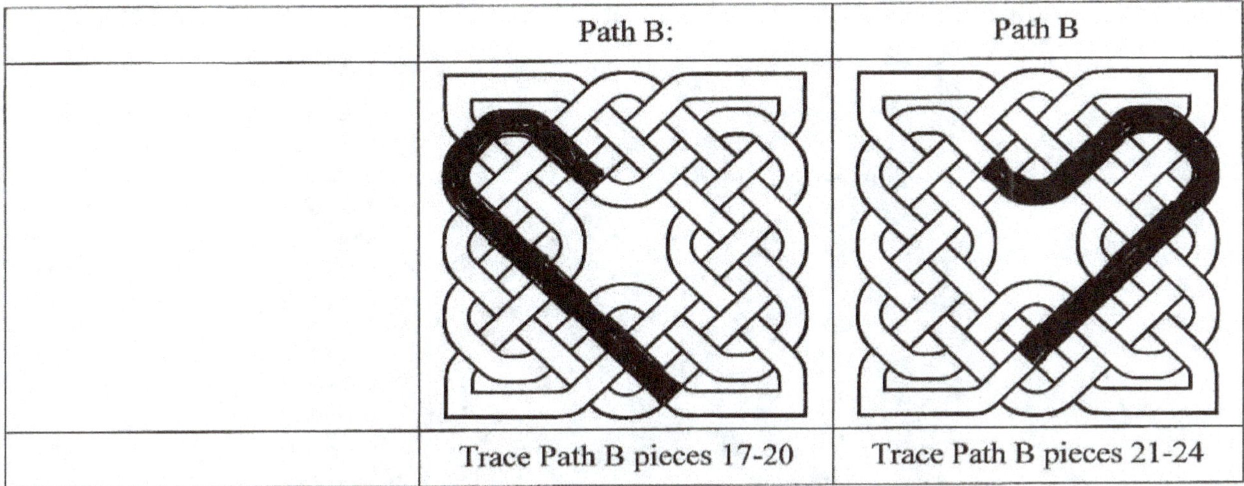

	Path B:	Path B
	Trace Path B pieces 17-20	Trace Path B pieces 21-24

1. Position Section 14-16 on the placement guide; position Section 17-20 on the placement guide on top of Section 14-16; position Path A on top of the juncture of Sections 14-16 and 17-20; position Section 1-3 on top of Path A. Fasten the path intersections to the placement guide along the bottom of the knot to anchor them in place where indicated.

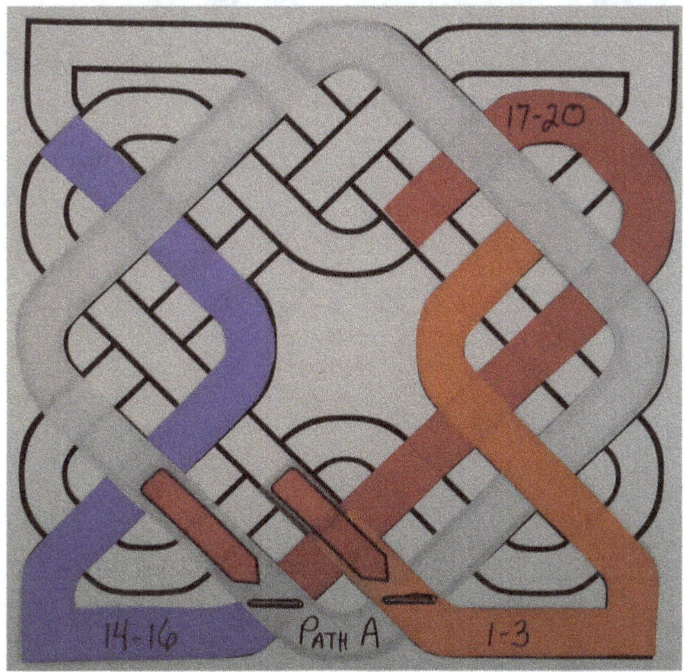

2. At the top of the knot, cut Path A where indicated (the cut ends are tucked under later).

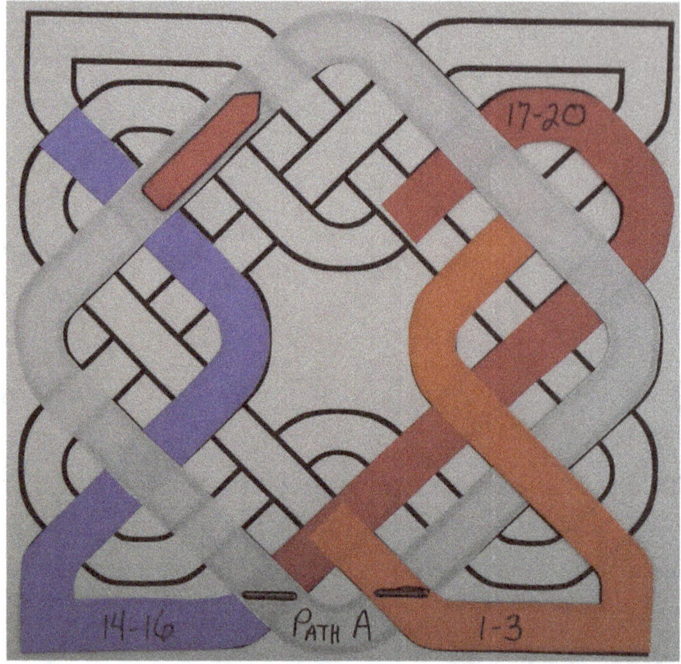

3. Lift Section 17-20 out of the way. Position Section 21-24 on the placement guide. Lay down
   Section 17-20. Fasten path intersection where indicated.

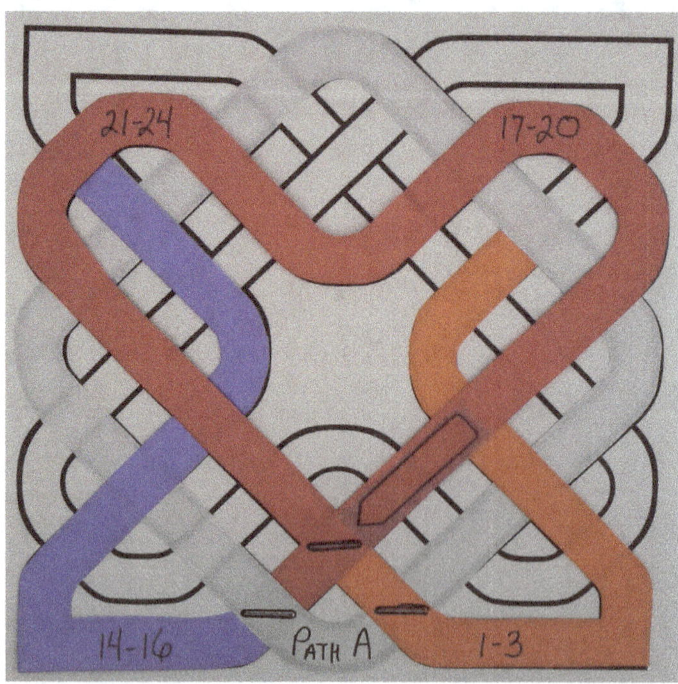

4. Lift Sections 14-16, 21-24 and the right end of Path A out of the way. Position Section 7-10 on the placement guide. Lay down Sections 14-16, 21-24 and the right end of Path A. Fasten path intersections where indicated.

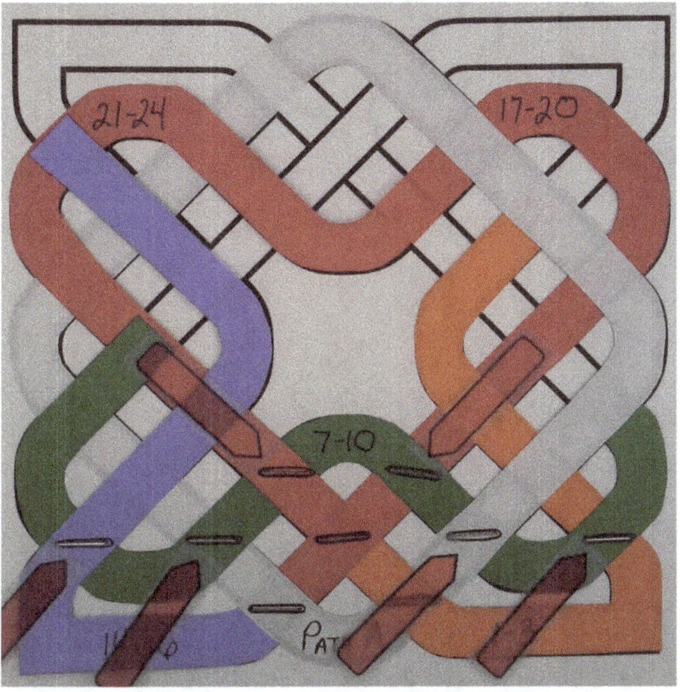

5. Lift Sections 7-10, 14-16, 21-24, and Path A out of the way. Lay down Section 21-24, then Section 14-16, then Path A, and then Section 7-10, tucking end under Section 21-24. Fasten path intersections where indicated.

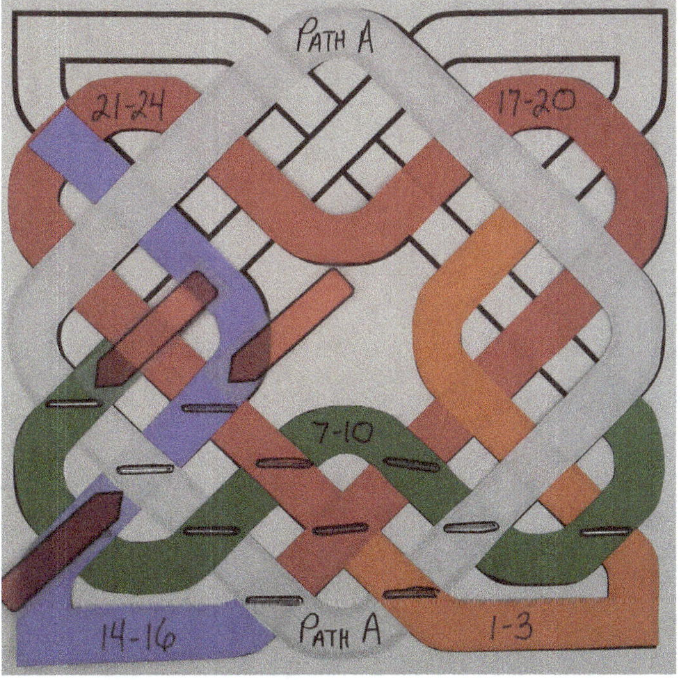

6. Lift Section 21-24, and Path A out of the way. Position Section 4-6 on the placement guide. Lay down Section 21-24, and then lay down Path A. Fasten path intersections where indicated.

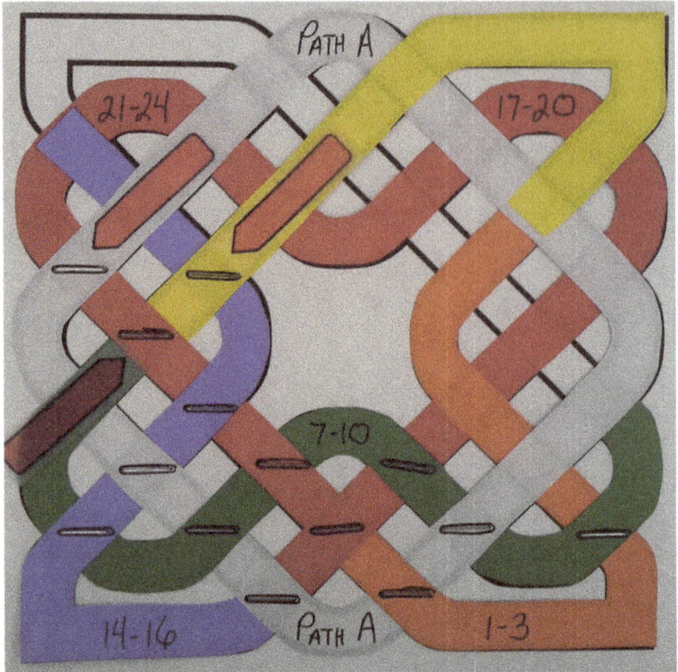

7. Lift Section 1-3 and the right end of Path A out of the way. Position Section 11-13 on the placement guide. Lay down Path A, and then Section 1-3. Fasten path intersections where indicated.

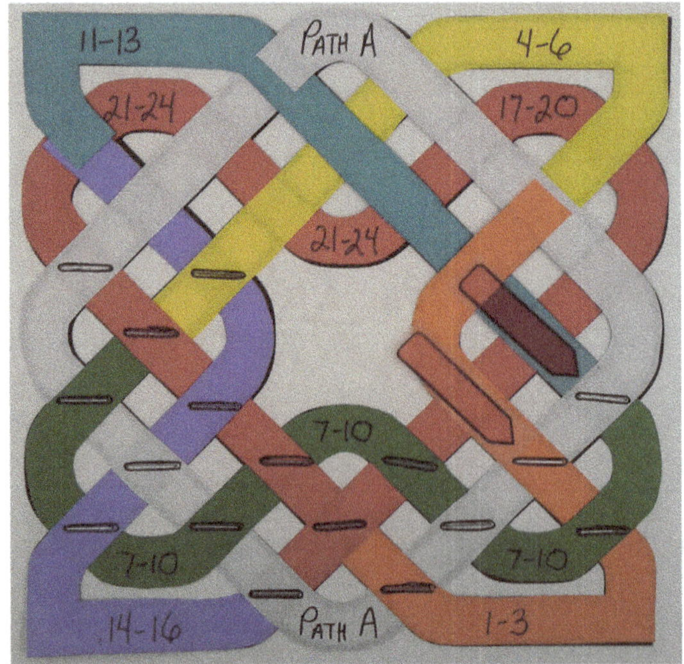

8. Lift Sections 1-3, 11-13, and 17-20 out of the way. Lay down Section 1-3, then Section 17-20, and then Section 11-13. Fasten path intersections where indicated.

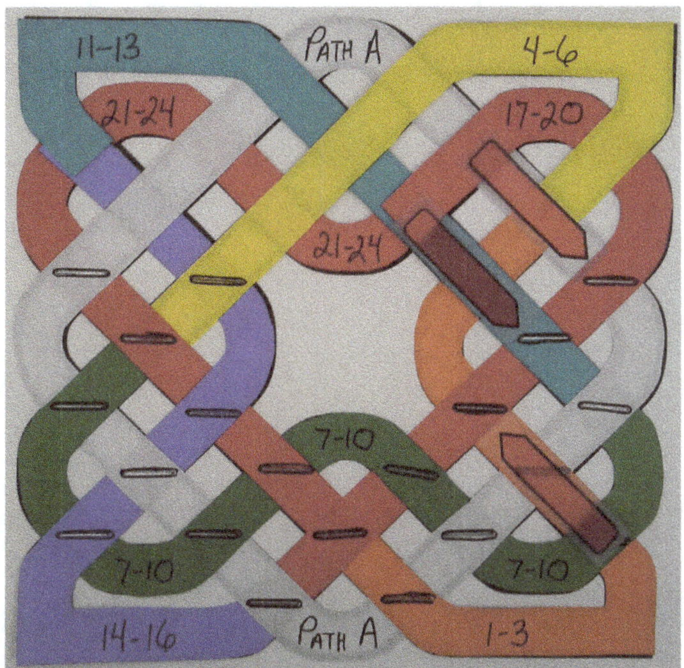

9. Lift Sections 1-3, 17-20, and Path A out of the way. Lay down Section 1-3, then Path A, and then Section 17-20, tucking end under Section 11-13. Fasten path intersections where indicated.

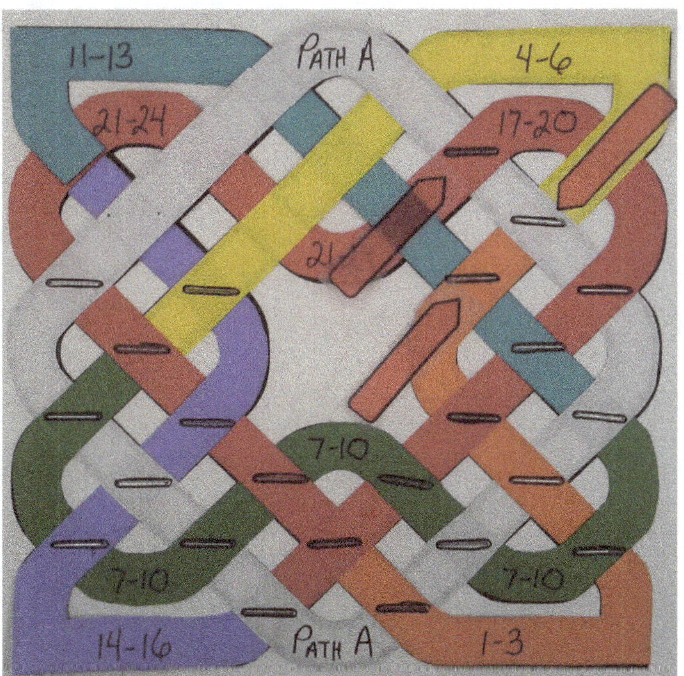

10. Lift Sections 11-13, 14-16, 21-24, and Path A out of the way. Lay down Path A, then Section 11-13, then Section 14-16, and then Section 21-24. Fasten path intersections where indicated.

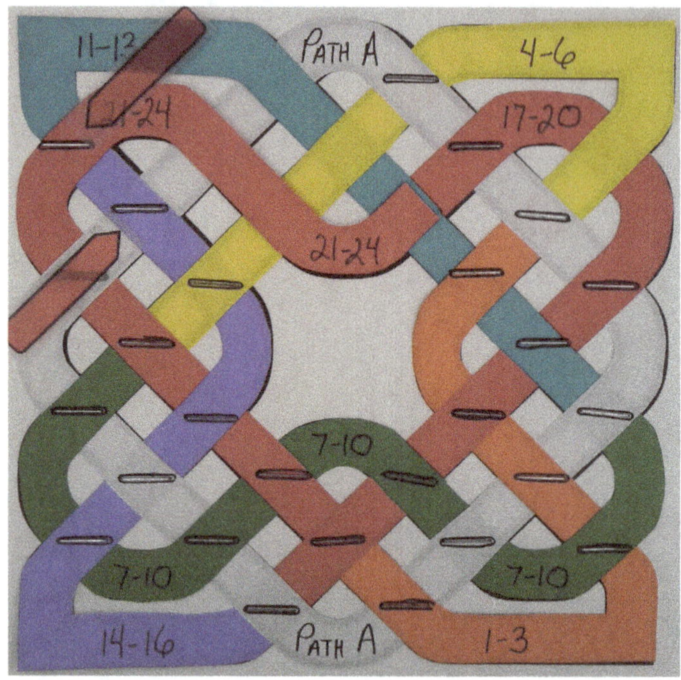

11. Lift Section 21-24 and Path A out of the way. Lay down Section 21-24, tucking end under Section 11-13; then lay down Path A, tucking end under Section 11-13. Fasten path intersections where indicated.

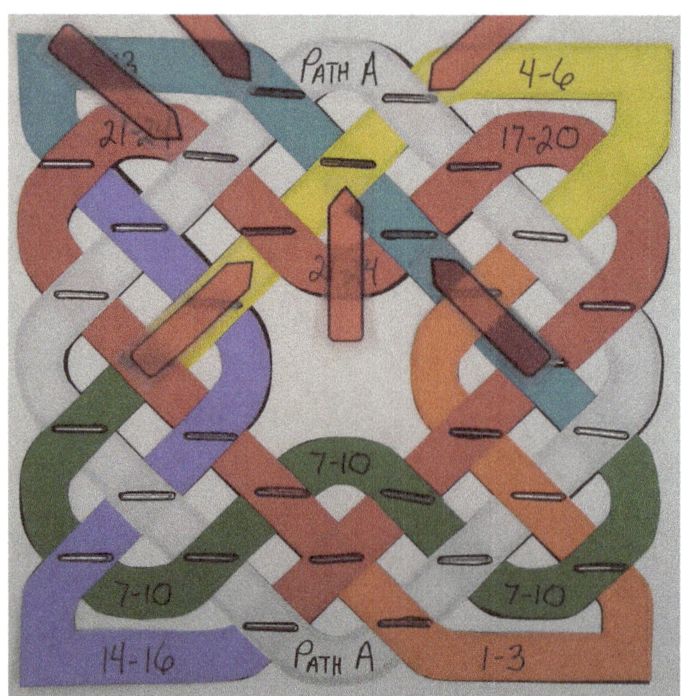

Celtic Knot #7

For this knot, I divided Path B into fourths.

Trace the outline of Path A.
Trace Path B, pieces 1 to 6.
Trace Path B, pieces 7 to 12.
Trace Path B, pieces 13 to 18.
Trace Path B, pieces 19 to 24.

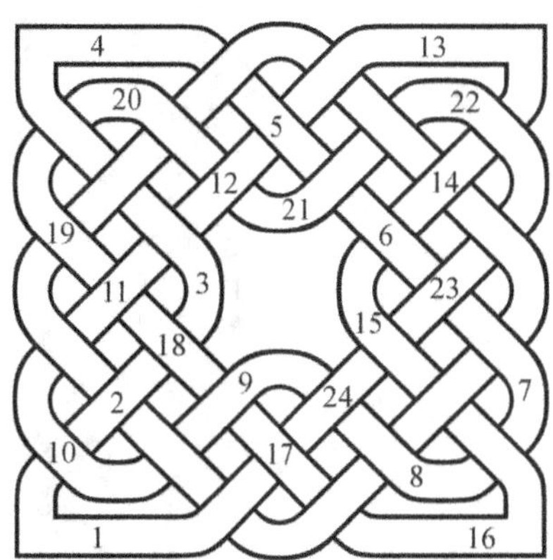

Path A:	Path B:	Path B:
Trace Path A	Trace Path B pieces 1-6	Trace Path B pieces 7-12

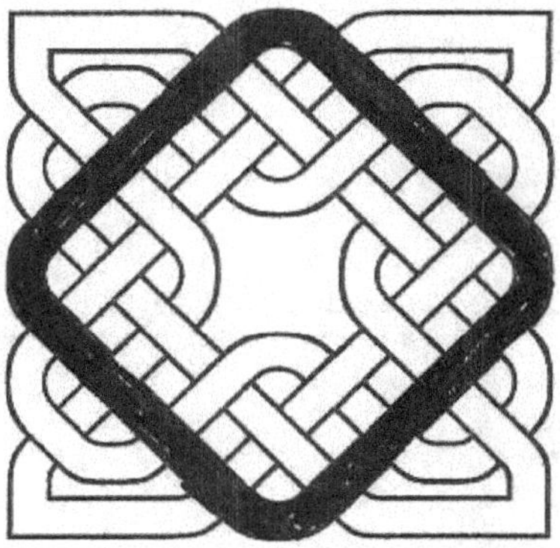

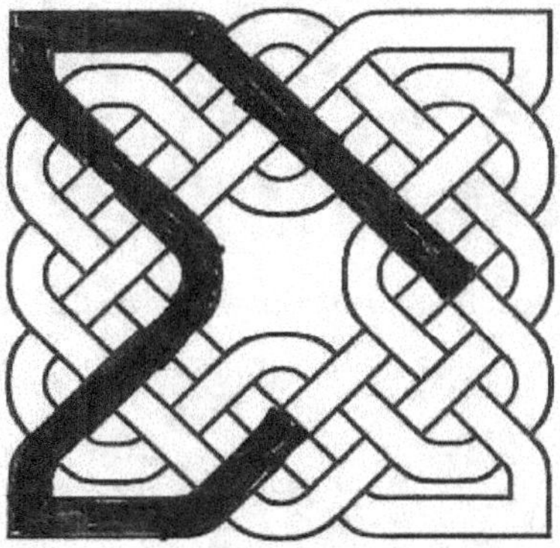

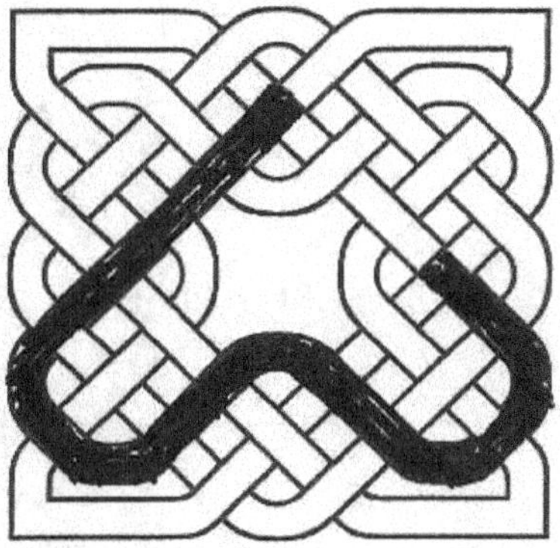

	Path B:	Path B:
	Trace Path B pieces 13-18	Trace Path B pieces 19-24

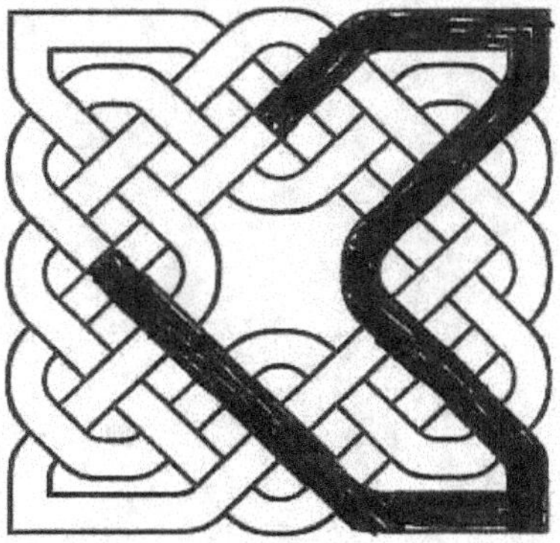

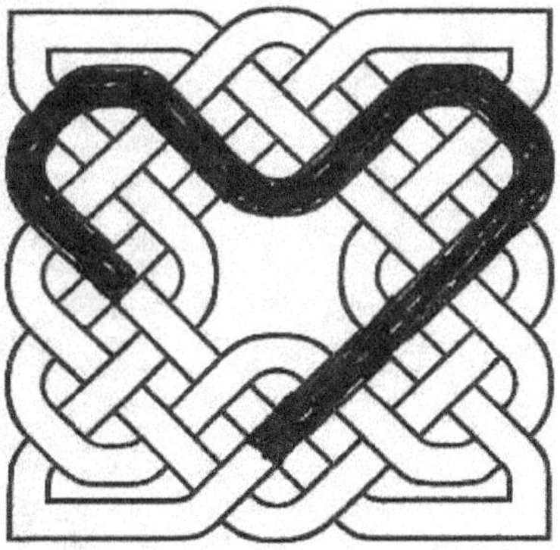

1. Position Section 13-18 on the placement guide; position Path A on top of Section 13-18; position Section 1-6 on top of Path A. Fasten the path intersections to the placement guide along the bottom of the knot to anchor them in place where indicated.

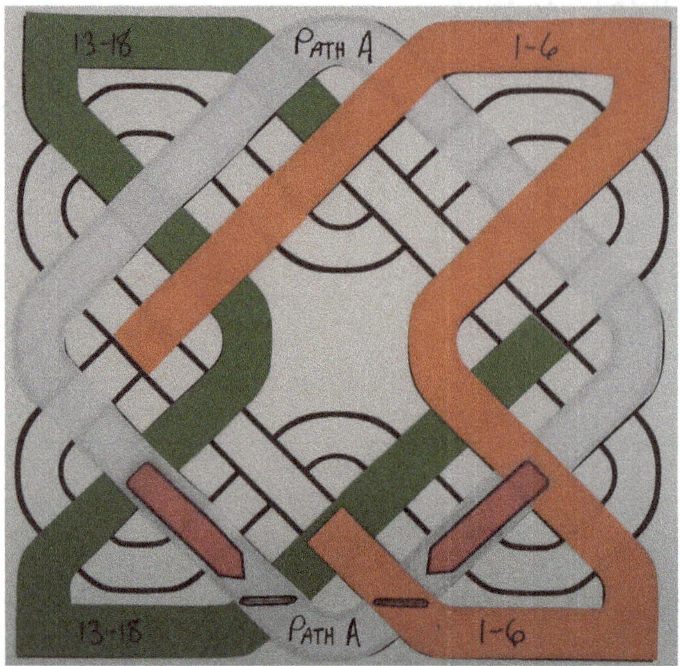

2. At the top of the knot, cut Path A where indicated (the cut ends are tucked under later).

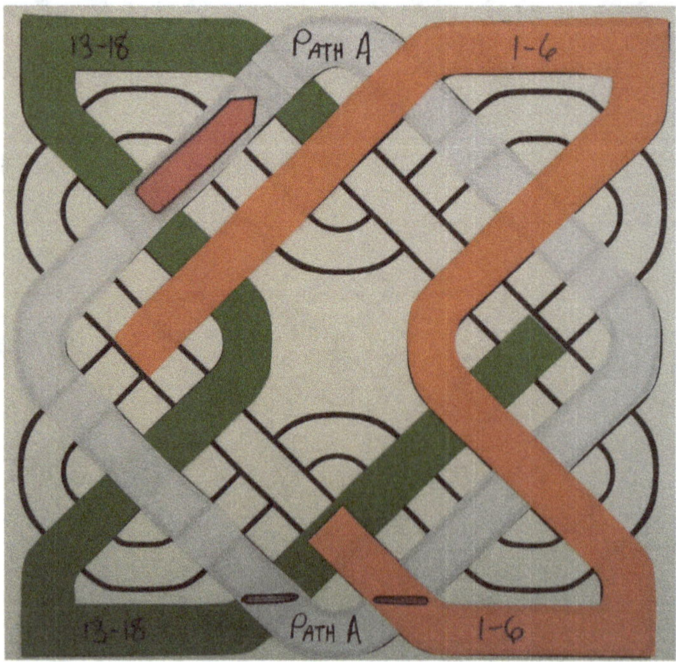

3. Lift right end of Section 13-18 out of the way. Position Section 19-24 on the placement guide. Lay down right end of Section 13-18. Fasten path intersection where indicated.

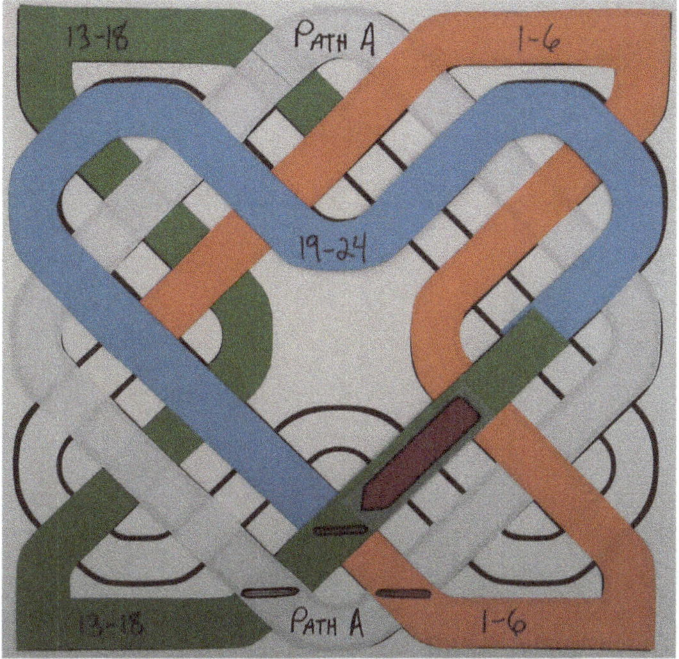

4. Lift left ends of Sections 13-18, 19-24, and right end of Path A out of the way. Position Section 7-12 on the placement guide. Lay down left ends of Sections 13-18, 19-24, and right end of Path A. Fasten path intersections where indicated.

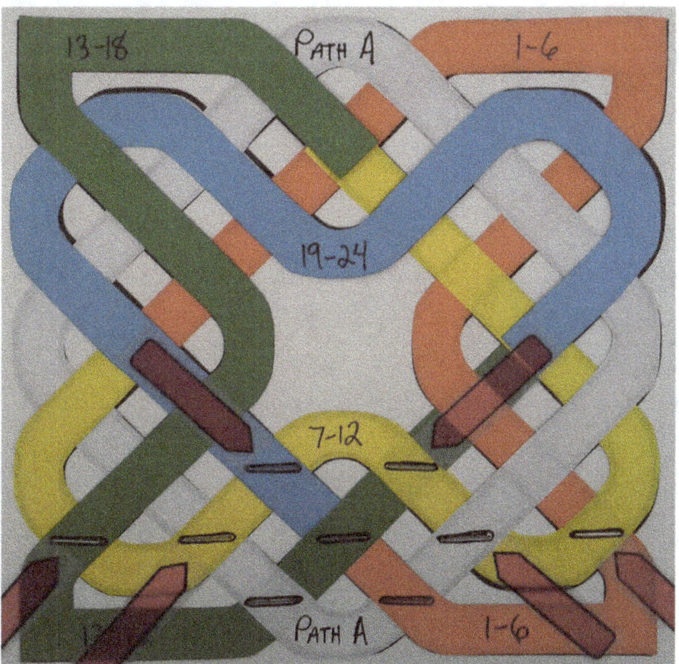

5. Lift left ends of Sections 7-12, 13-18, and Path A out of the way. Lay down Section 13-18, then Path A, then Section 7-12, tucking the end under Section 19-24. Fasten path intersections where indicated.

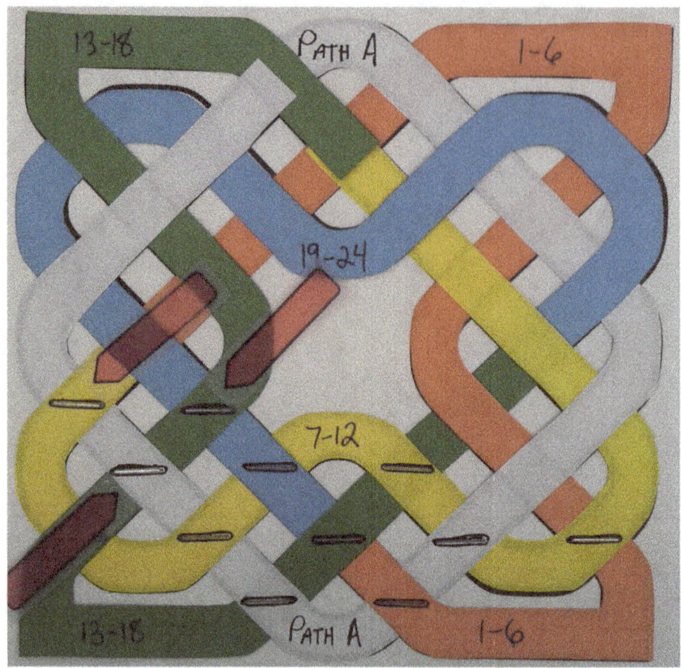

6. Lift right ends of Sections 1-6, 13-18, and Path A out of the way. Lay down Path A, then Section 1-6, and then Section 13-18, tucking the end under Section 7-12. Fasten path intersections where indicated.

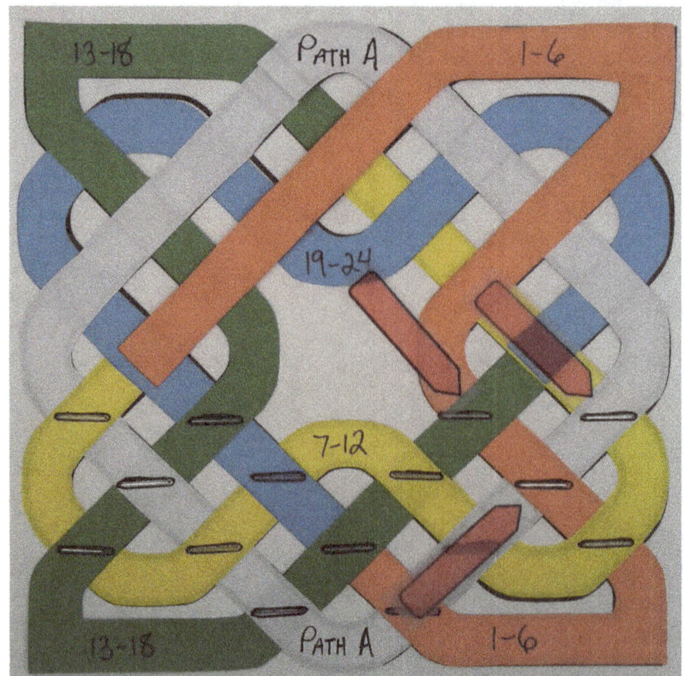

7. Sections 1-6 and 19-24 pose a problem: their cut ends lie on opposite sides of the knot's vertical dividing line. Cut Sections 1-6 and 19-24 where indicated (the cut ends are tucked under later).

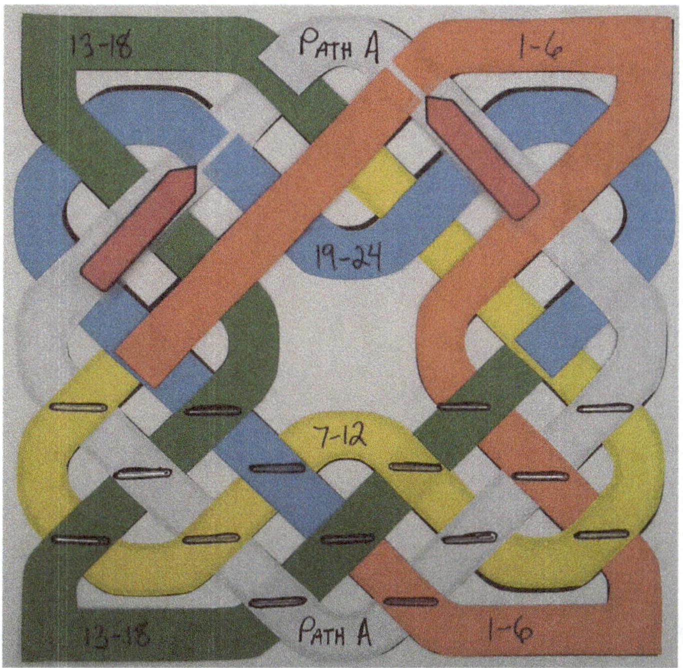

8. Lift right ends of Sections 1-6, and 7-12 out of the way. Lay down cut section of Section 19-24, then Section 7-12, and then Section 1-6. Fasten path intersections where indicated.

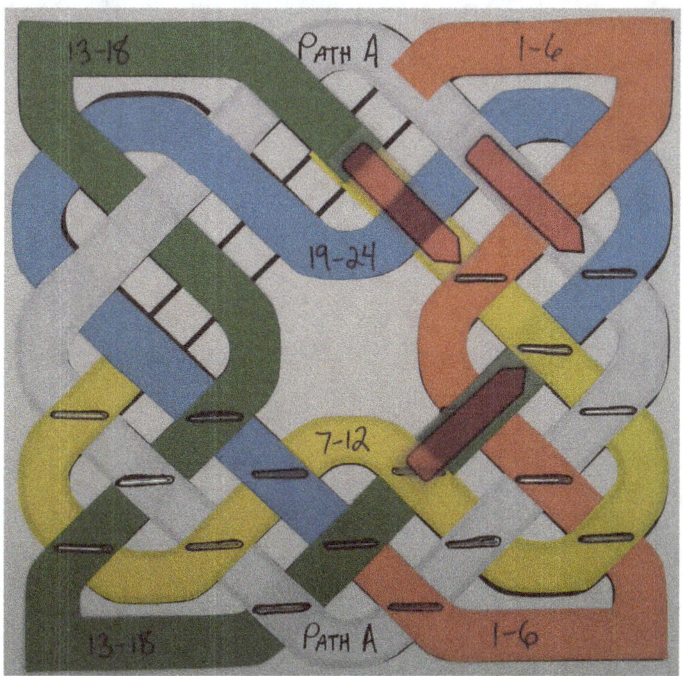

9. Lift left ends of Section 19-24 and Path A out of the way. Position cut section of Section 1-6 on the placement guide. Lay down Section 19-24, and then Path A. Fasten path intersections where indicated.

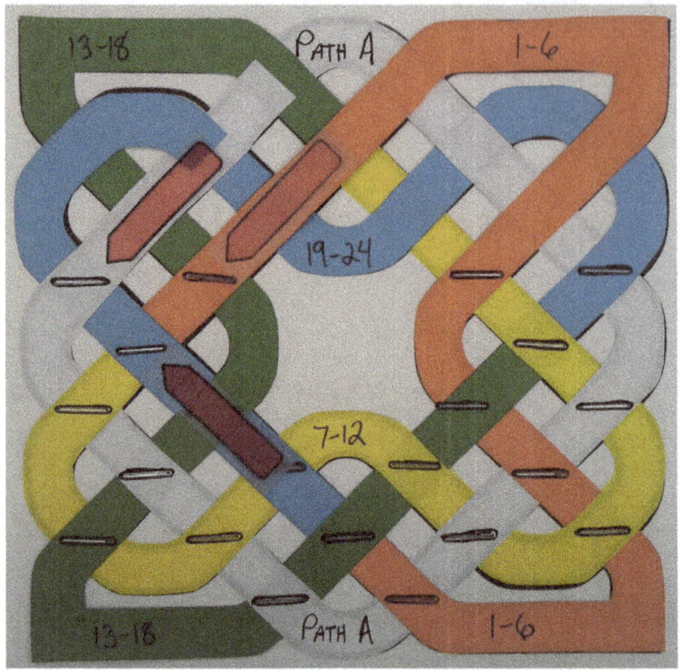

10. Lift left ends of Sections 13-18, 19-24, and Path A out of the way. Lay down Path A, then Section 13-18, and then Section 19-24, tucking end under Path A. Fasten path intersections where indicated.

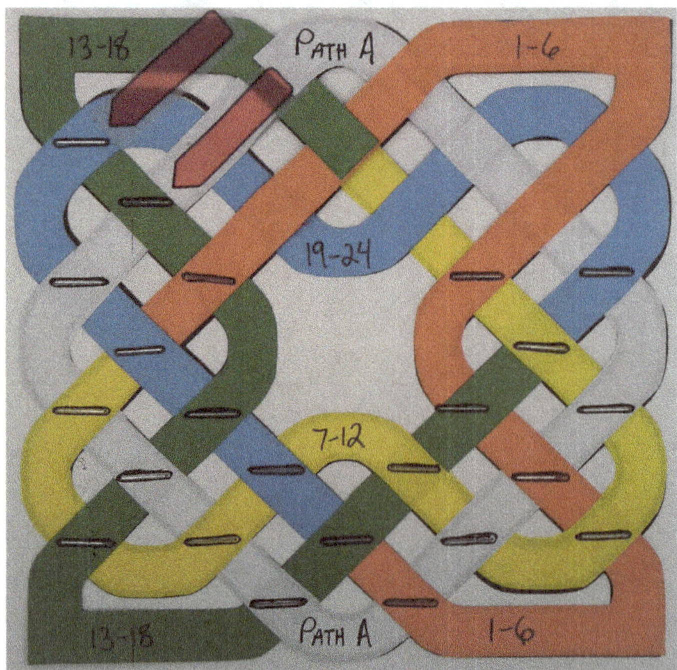

11. Lift right ends of Section 1-6 and Path A out of the way. Lay down Section 1-6, then Path A. Fasten path intersections where indicated.

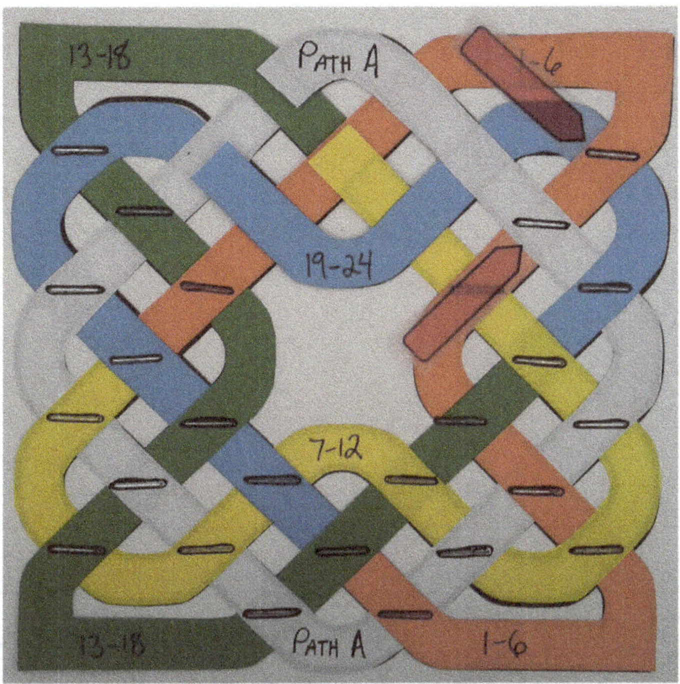

12. Lift right ends of Sections 7-12, 19-24, and Path A out of the way. Lay down Path A, tucking end under Section 13-18; then lay down Section 19-24, tucking end under Path A; and then lay down Section 7-12, tucking end under Section 1-6. Fasten path intersections where indicated.

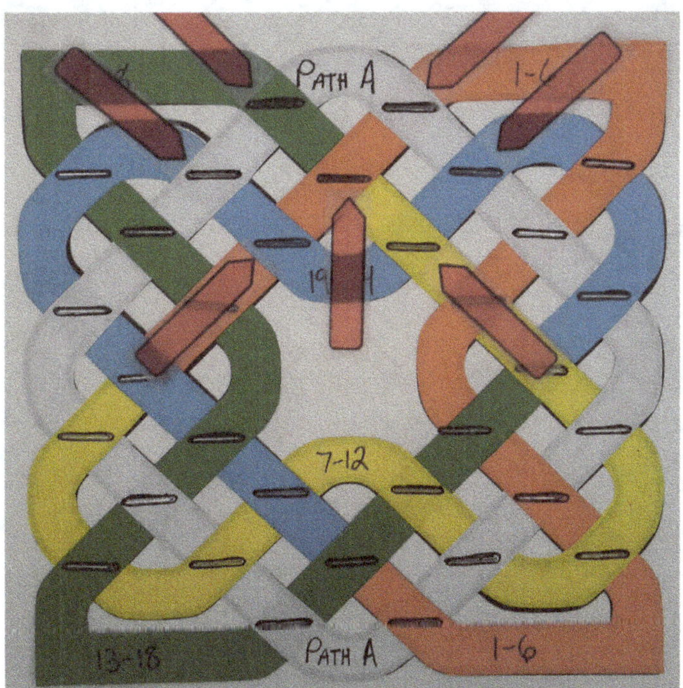

Celtic Knot #8

This time, I divided Path B into fifths (one section has one piece less than the other four).

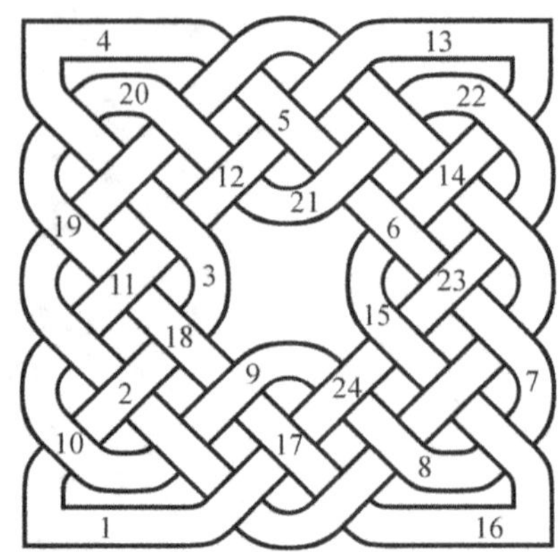

Trace the outline of Path A.
Trace Path B, pieces 1 to 5.
Trace Path B, pieces 6 to 10.
Trace Path B, pieces 11 to 14.
Trace Path B, pieces 15 to 19.
Trace Path B, pieces 20 to 24.

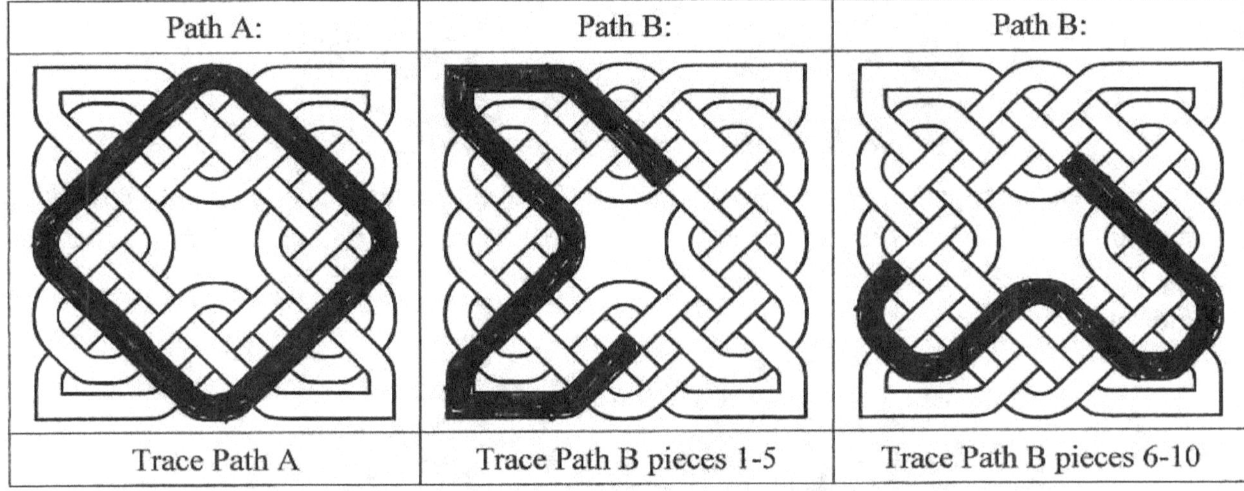

Path A:	Path B:	Path B:
Trace Path A	Trace Path B pieces 1-5	Trace Path B pieces 6-10

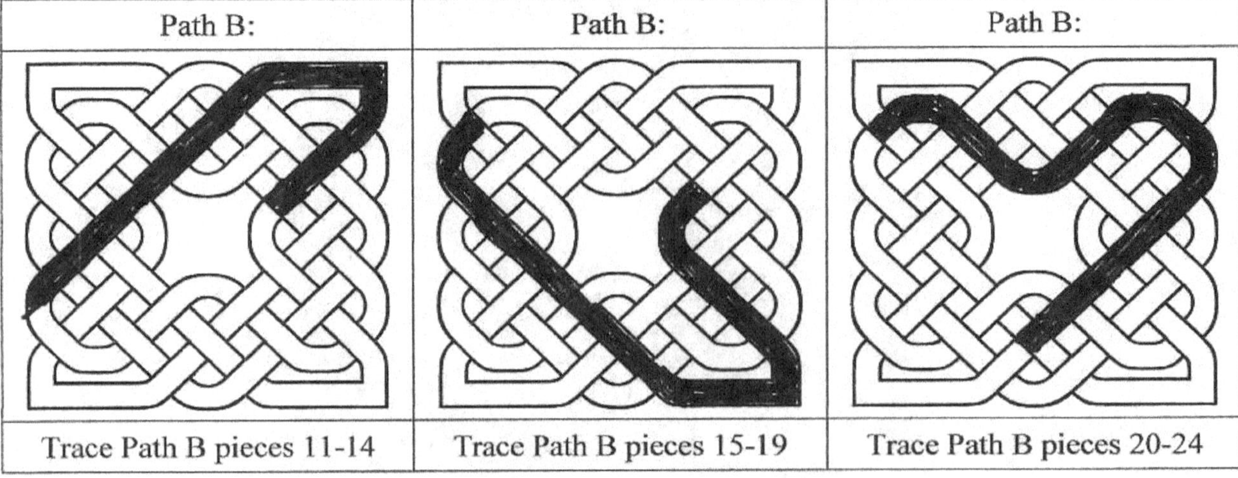

Path B:	Path B:	Path B:
Trace Path B pieces 11-14	Trace Path B pieces 15-19	Trace Path B pieces 20-24

1. Position Section 15-19 on the placement guide; position Path A on top of Section 15-19; position Section 1-5 on top of Path A. Fasten the path intersections to the placement guide along the bottom of the knot to anchor them in place where indicated.

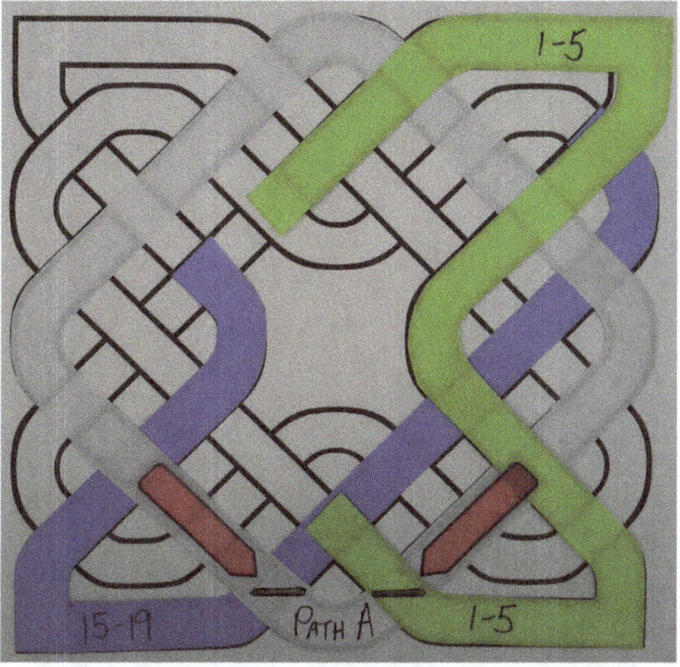

2. At the top of the knot, cut Path A where indicated (the cut ends are tucked under later).

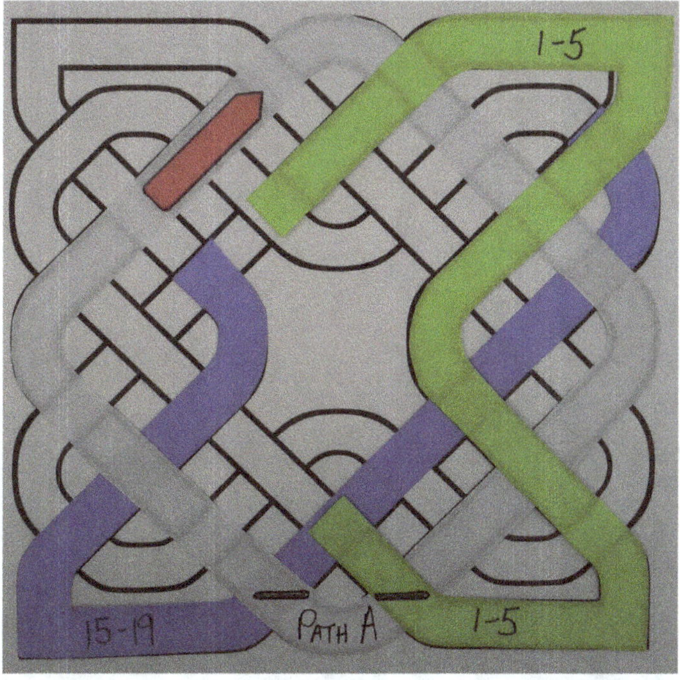

3. Lift right end of Section 15-19 out of the way. Position Section 20-24 on the placement guide. Lay down right end of Section 15-19. Fasten path intersection where indicated.

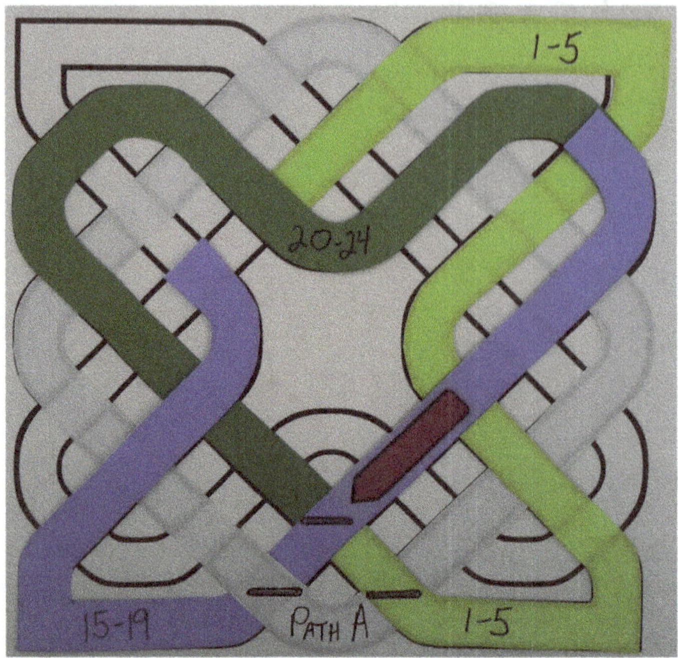

4. Lift left ends of Sections 15-19, 20-24, and right end of Path A out of the way. Position Section 6-10 on the placement guide. Lay down left ends of Sections 15-19, 20-24, and right end of Path A. Fasten path intersections where indicated.

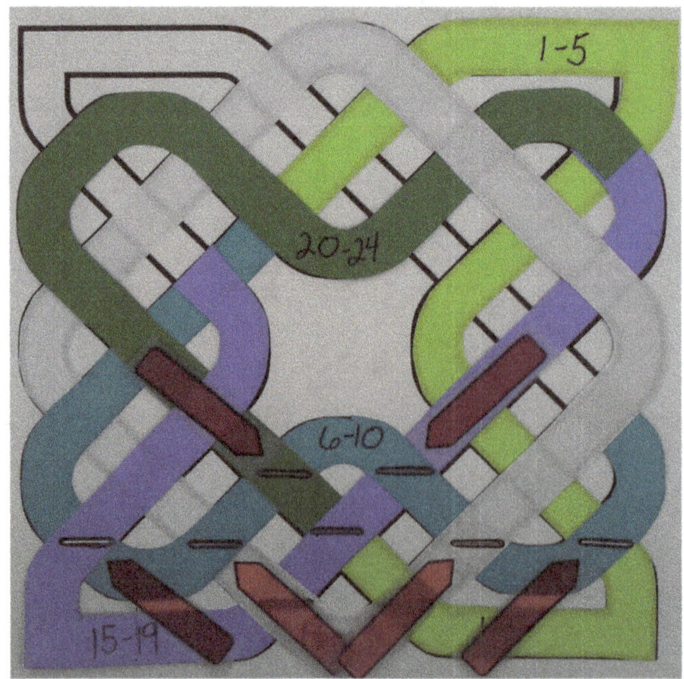

5. Lift left ends of Sections 15-19, 6-10, and Path A out of the way. Lay down Section 15-19, then Path A, and then Section 6-10. Fasten path intersections where indicated.

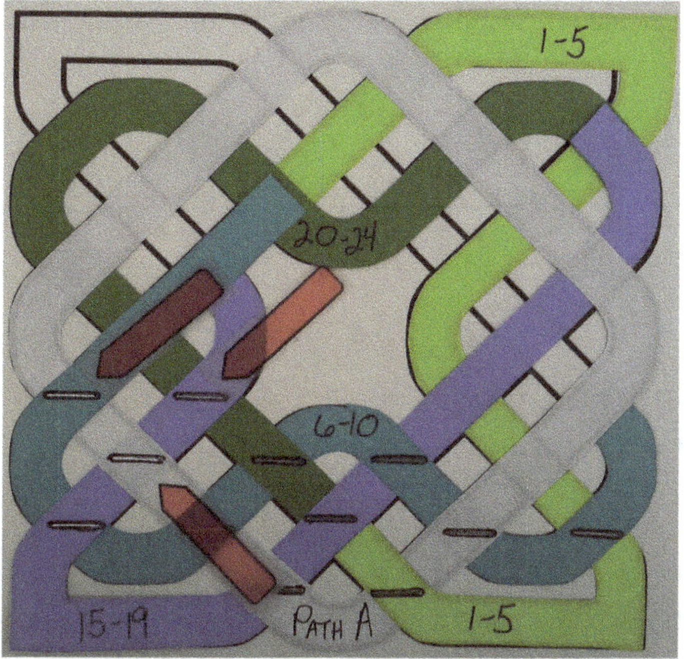

6. Lift left ends of Sections 6-10, 20-24, and Path A out of the way. Lay down Section 6-10, then Section 20-24, and then Path A. Fasten path intersections where indicated.

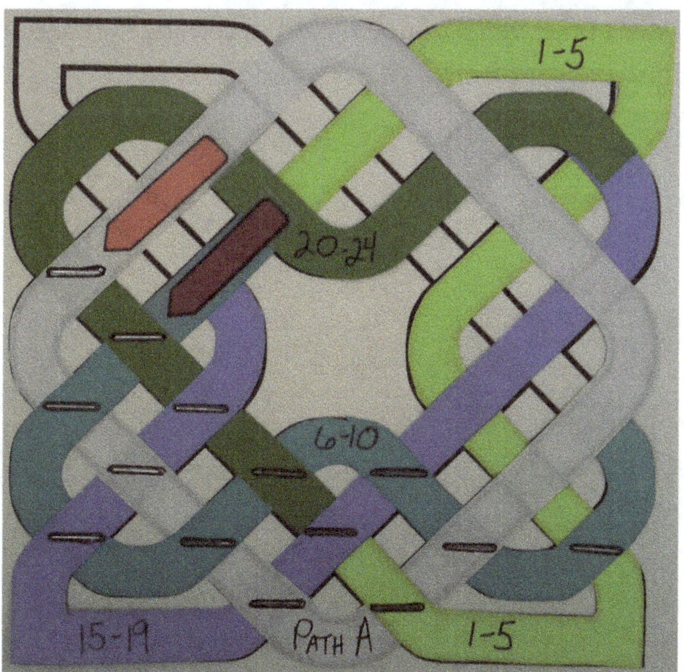

7. Lift left ends of Sections 6-10 and 20-24 out of the way. Position section 11-14 on the placement guide. Lay down Sections 6-10 and 20-24. Fasten path intersections where indicated.

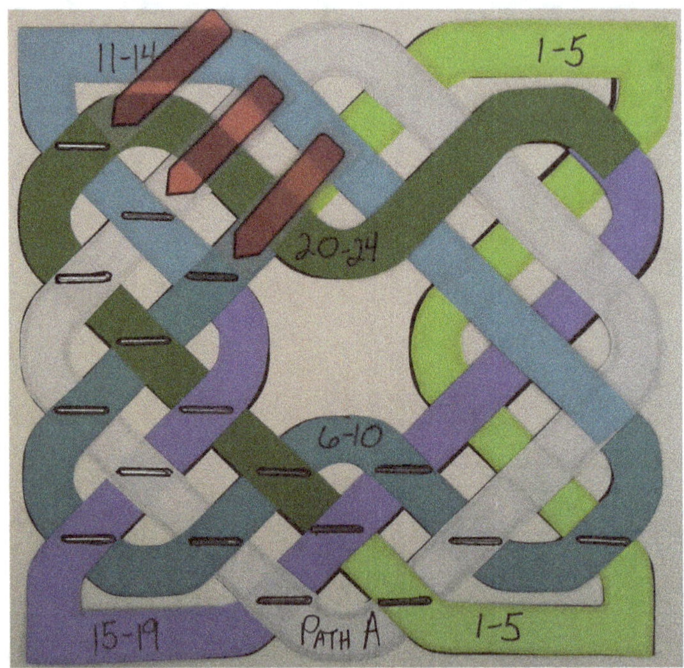

8. Lift left end of Path A out of the way. Lay down Path A, tucking end under Section 11-14. Fasten path intersection where indicated.

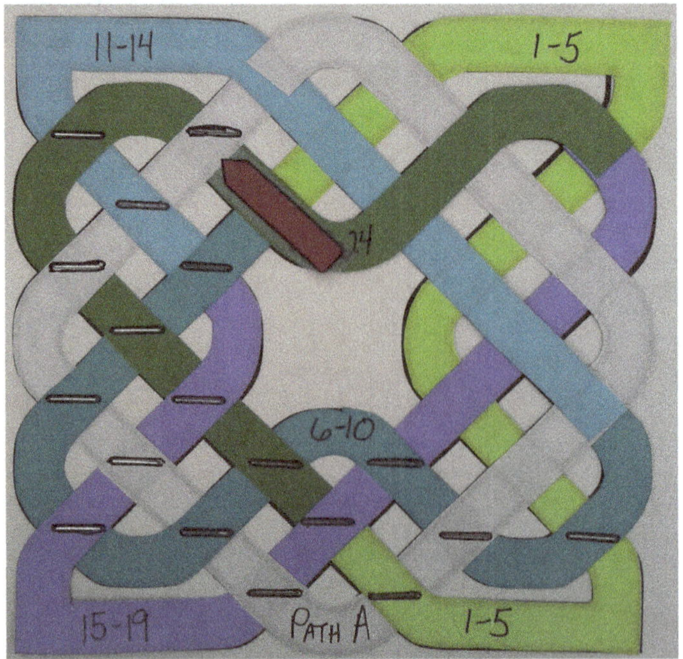

9. Cut Section 11-14 where indicated.

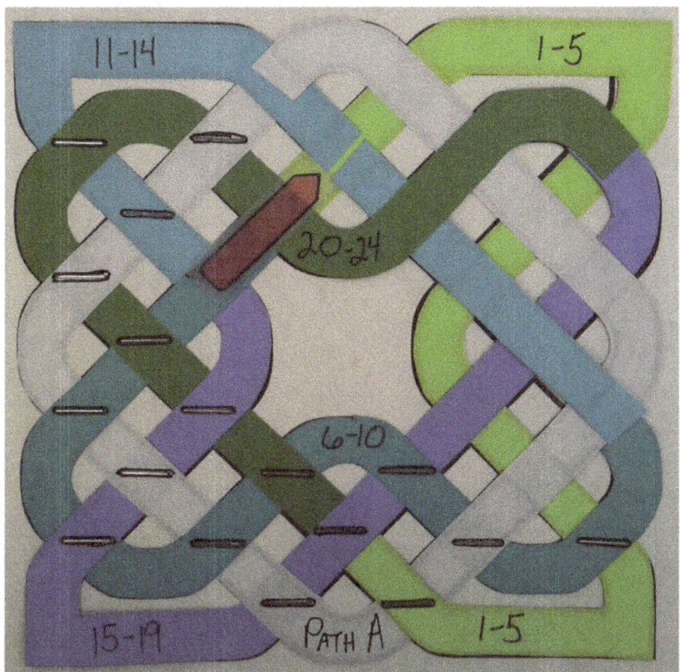

10. Lift right ends of Sections 1-5, 6-10, and Path A out of the way. Lay down Path A, then Section 1-5, and then Section 15-19. Fasten path intersections where indicated.

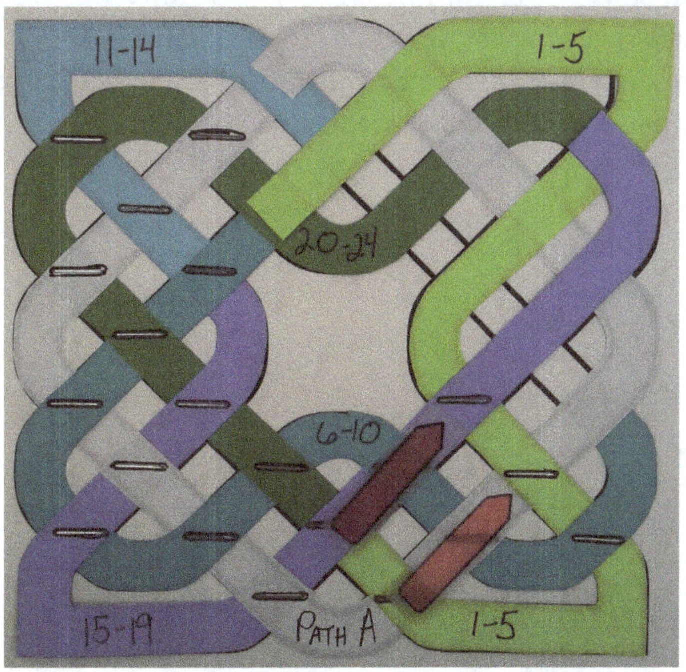

11. Lift right ends of Section 1-5, and Path A. Position cut section of Section 11-14 on the placement guide. Lay down Section 1-5 and Path A. Fasten path intersections where indicated.

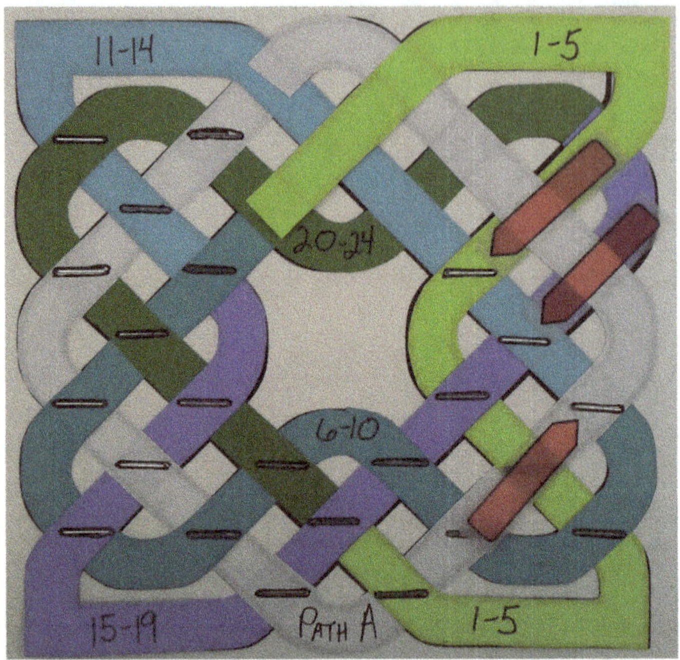

12. Lift right ends of Sections 1-5, 11-14, 15-19, 20-24, and Path A out of the way. Lay down Path A, tucking end under Section 11-14; then lay down Section 15-19, tucking end under Section 1-5; then lay down Section 20-24, tucking end under Section 1-5; and then lay down Section 11-14, tucking end under Section 1-5. Fasten path intersections where indicated.

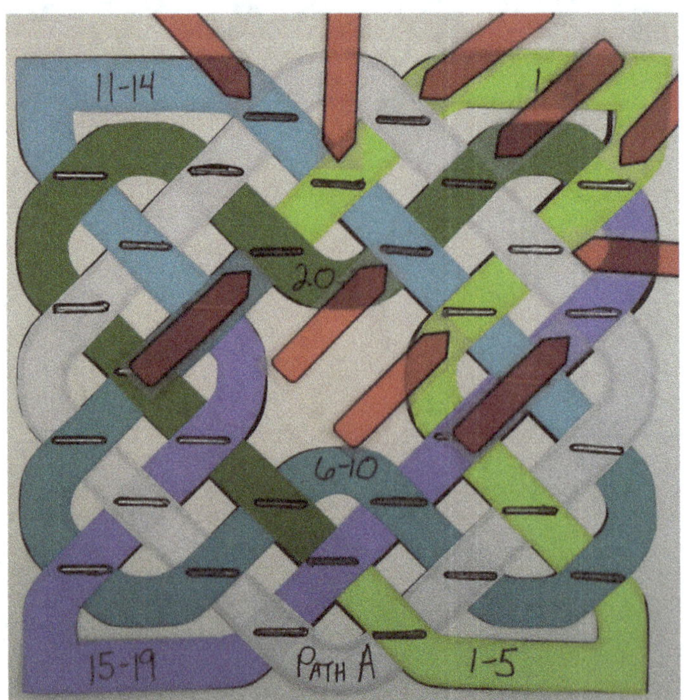

Celtic Knot #9

The ninth knot divides Path B into eighths.

Trace the outline of Path A.
Trace Path B, pieces 1 to 3.
Trace Path B, pieces 4 to 6.
Trace Path B, pieces 7 to 9.
Trace Path B, pieces 10 to 12.
Trace Path B, pieces 13 to 15.
Trace Path B, pieces 16 to 18.
Trace Path B, pieces 19 to 21.
Trace Path B, pieces 22 to 24.

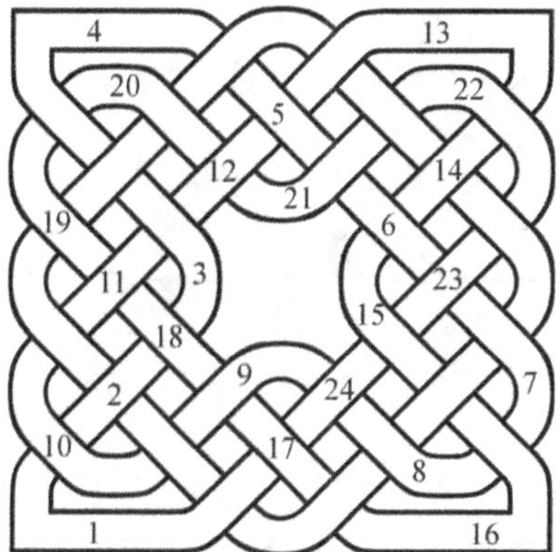

Path A:	Path B:	Path B
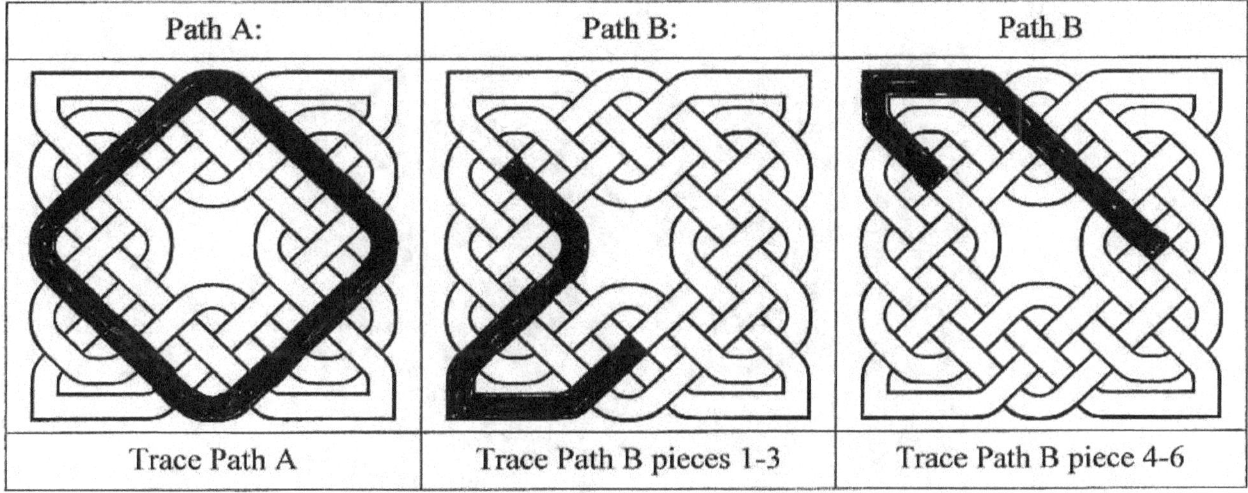		
Trace Path A	Trace Path B pieces 1-3	Trace Path B piece 4-6

Path B:	Path B:	Path B
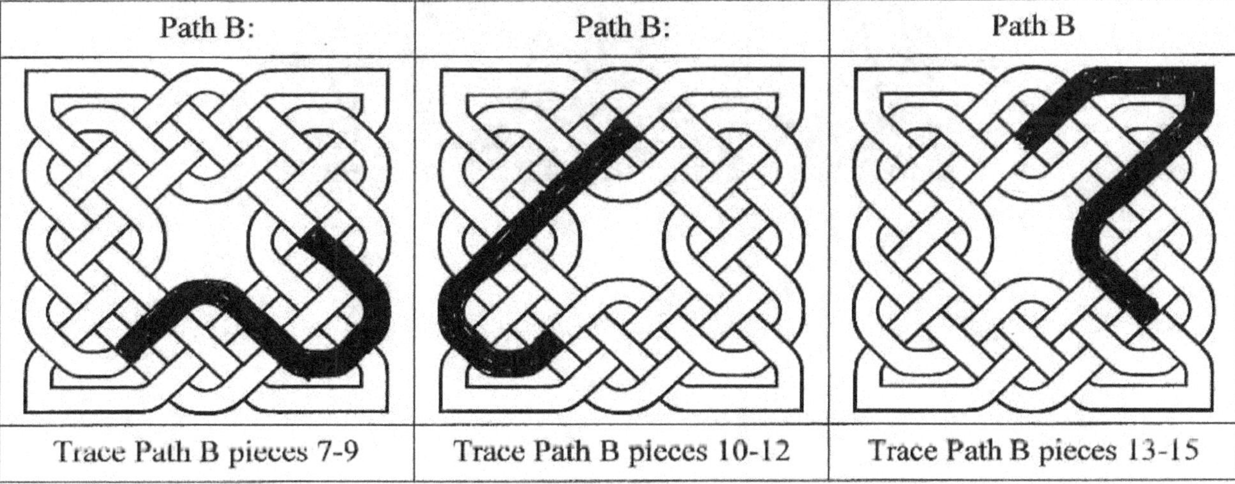		
Trace Path B pieces 7-9	Trace Path B pieces 10-12	Trace Path B pieces 13-15

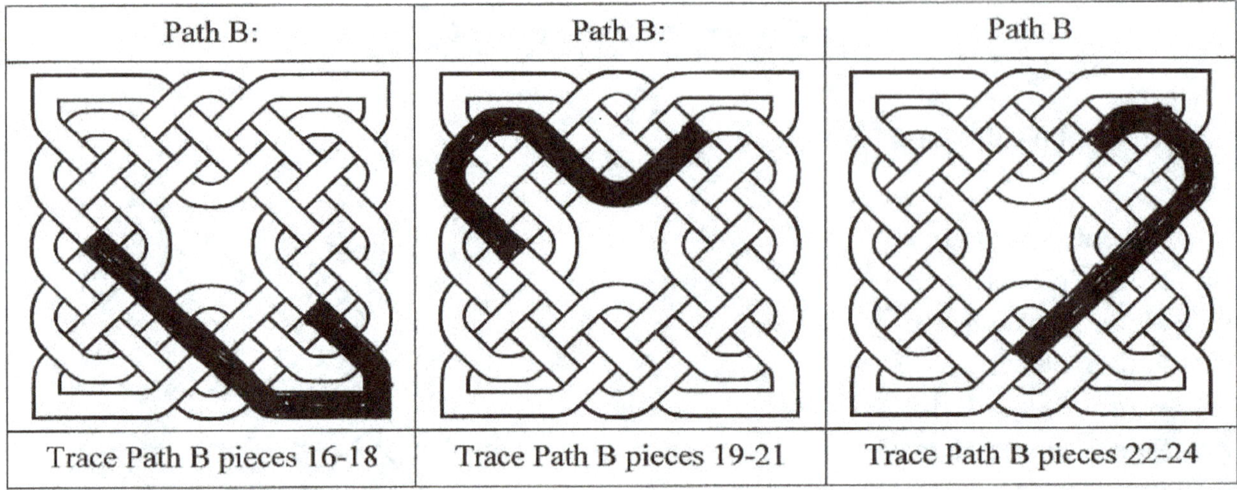

Path B:	Path B:	Path B
Trace Path B pieces 16-18	Trace Path B pieces 19-21	Trace Path B pieces 22-24

1. Position Section 16-18 on the placement guide; position Path A on top of Section 16-18; position Section 1-3 on top of Path A. Fasten the path intersections to the placement guide along the bottom of the knot to anchor them in place where indicated.

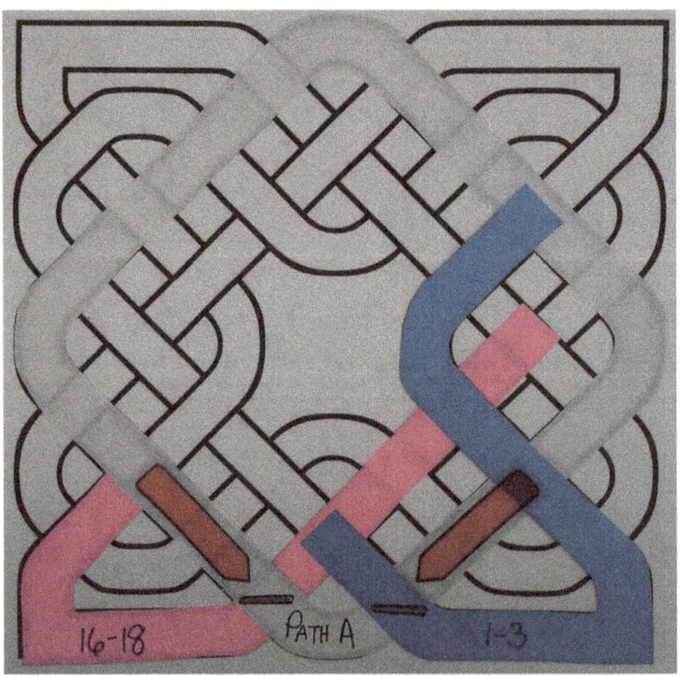

2. At the top of the knot, cut Path A where indicated (the cut ends are tucked under later).

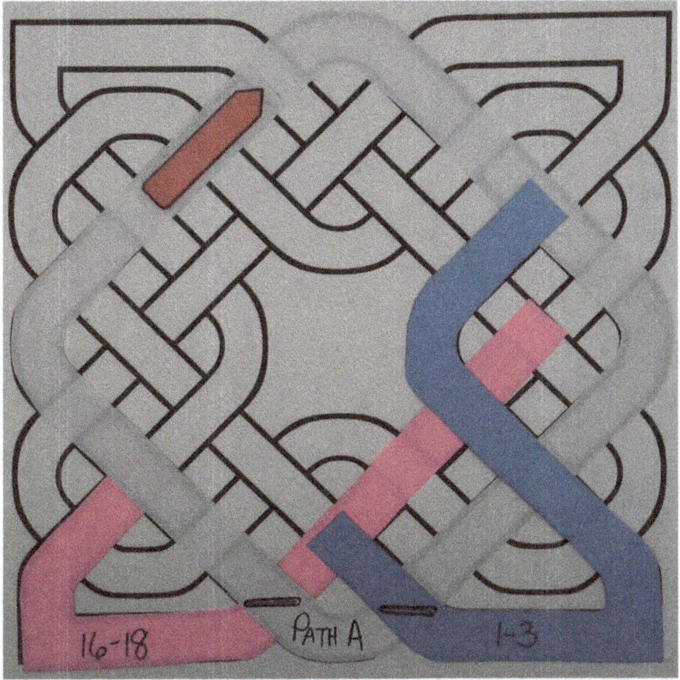

3. Lift right end of Section 16-18 out of the way. Position Section 22-24 on the placement guide. Lay down right end of Section 16-18. Fasten path intersection where indicated.

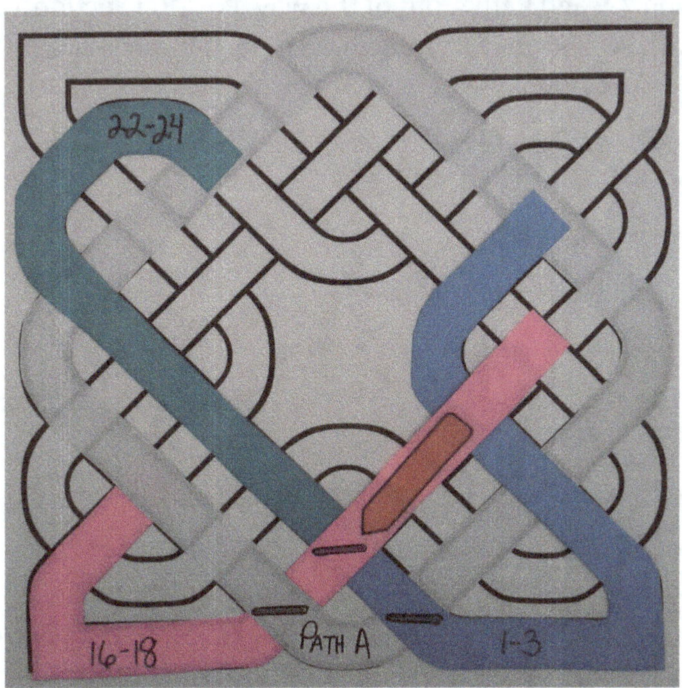

4. Lift left ends of Sections 16-18, and 22-24 out of the way. Position Section 7-9 on the placement guide. Lay down left ends of Sections 16-18, and 22-24. Fasten path intersections where indicated.

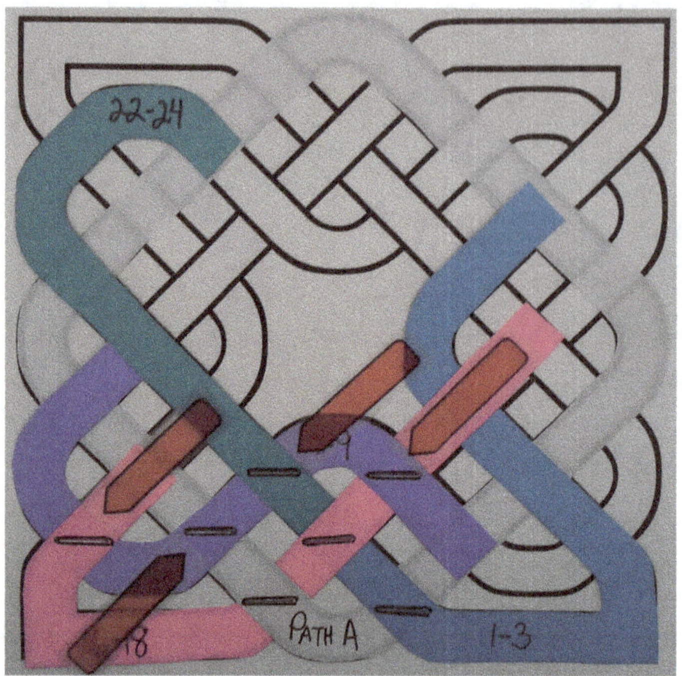

5. Lift left ends of Section 7-9 and Path A out of the way. Position Section 13-15 on the placement guide. Lay down Path A, and then lay down Section 7-9, tucking end under Section 22-24. Fasten path intersections where indicated.

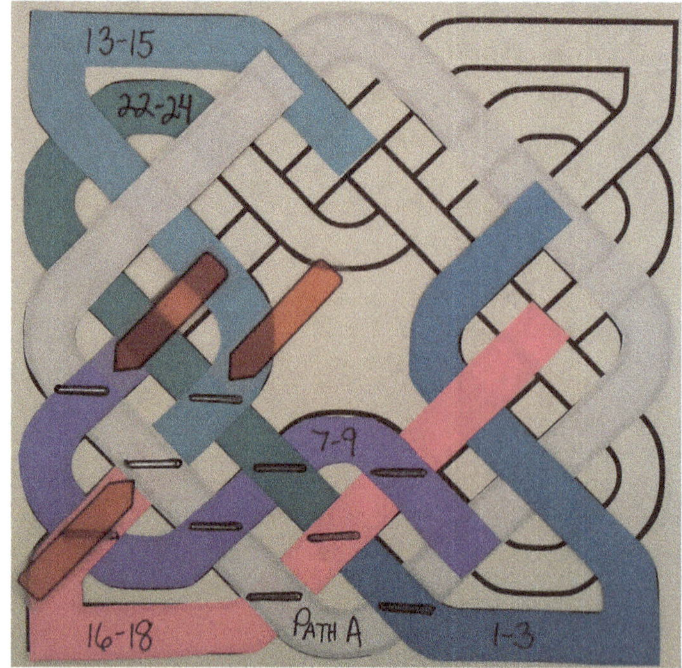

6. Lift left ends of Section 22-24 and Path A out of the way. Position Section 4-6 on the placement guide. Lay down Section 22-24, then Path A. Fasten path intersections where indicated.

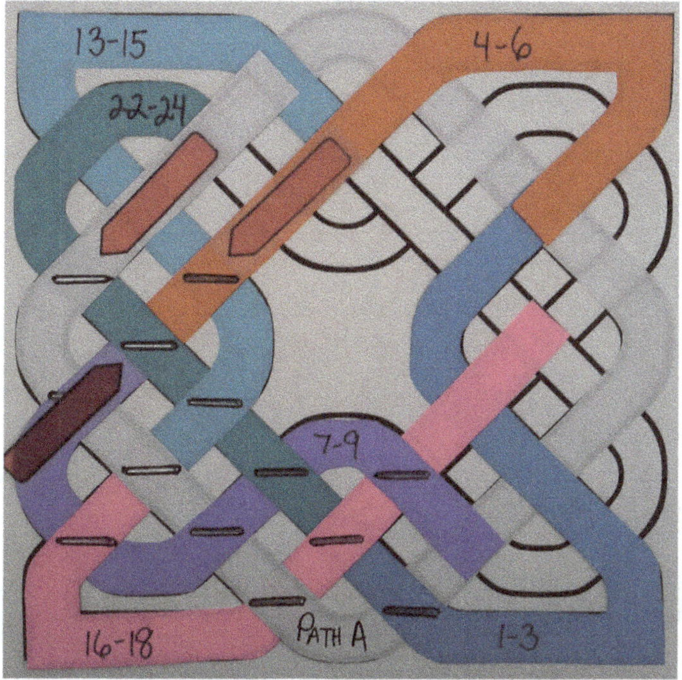

7. Lift right end of Path A out of the way. Position Section 10-12 on the placement guide. Lay down Path A. Fasten path intersections where indicated.

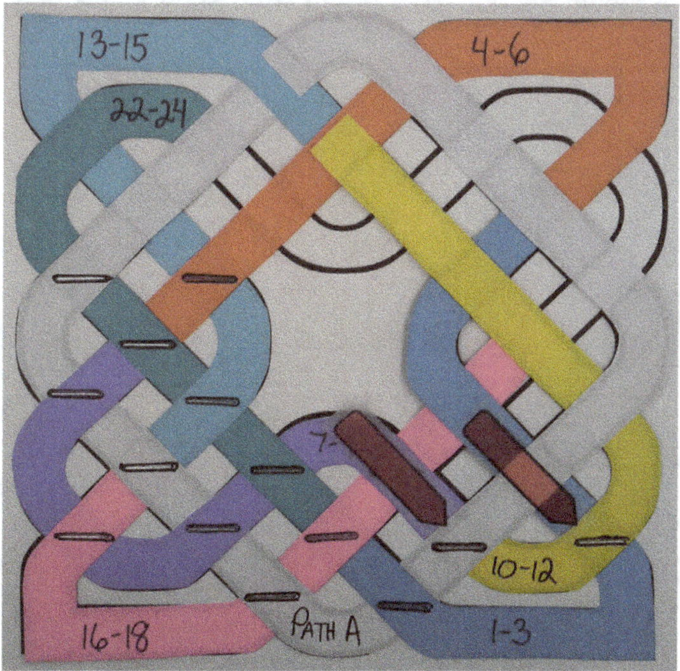

8. Lift right ends of Sections 1-3, 16-18, and Path A out of the way. Lay down Path A, then Section 1-3, and then Section 16-18, tucking end under Section 10-12. Fasten path intersections where indicated.

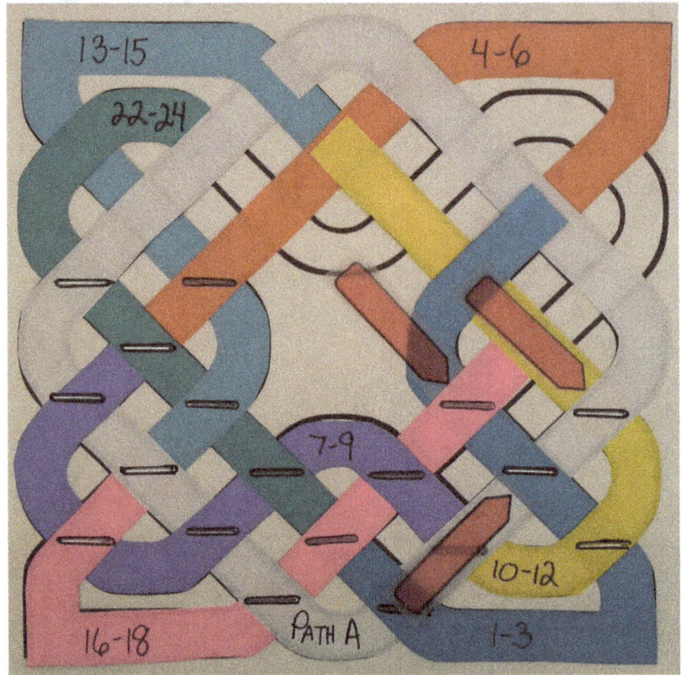

9. Lift ends of Sections 1-3, 4-6, and 10-12 out of the way. Position Section 19-21 on the placement guide. Lay down Section 10-12, and then Section 1-3. Fasten path intersections where indicated.

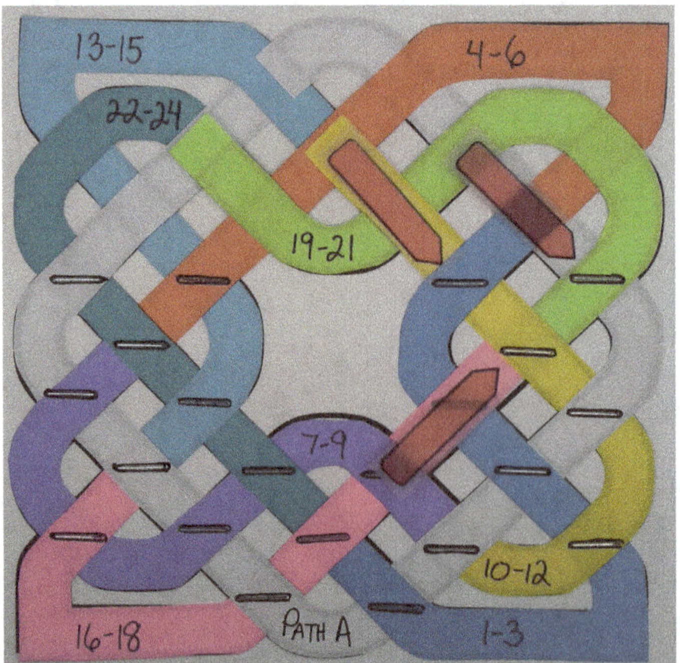

10. Lift ends of Sections 13-15, 22-24, and Path A out of the way. Lay down Path A, then Section 13-15, and then Section 22-24, tucking end under Path A. Fasten path intersections where indicated.

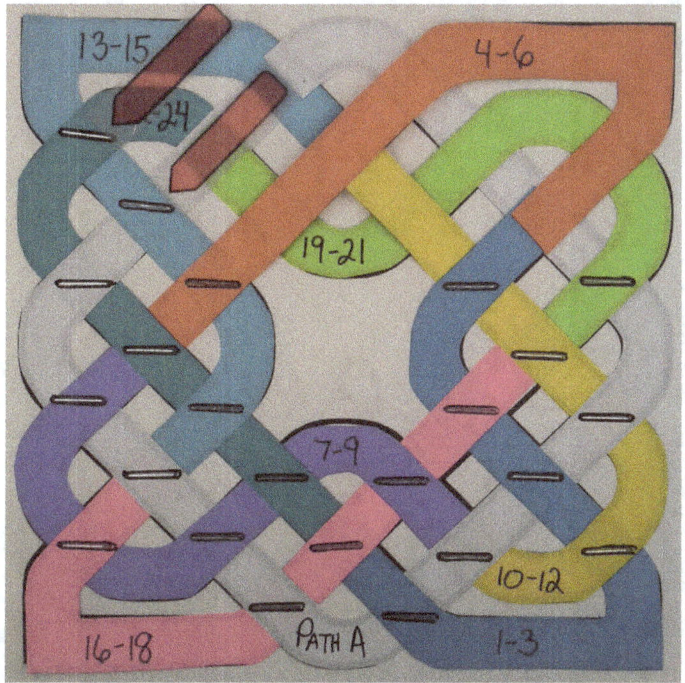

11. Cut Section 4-6 where indicated (the cut ends are tucked under later).

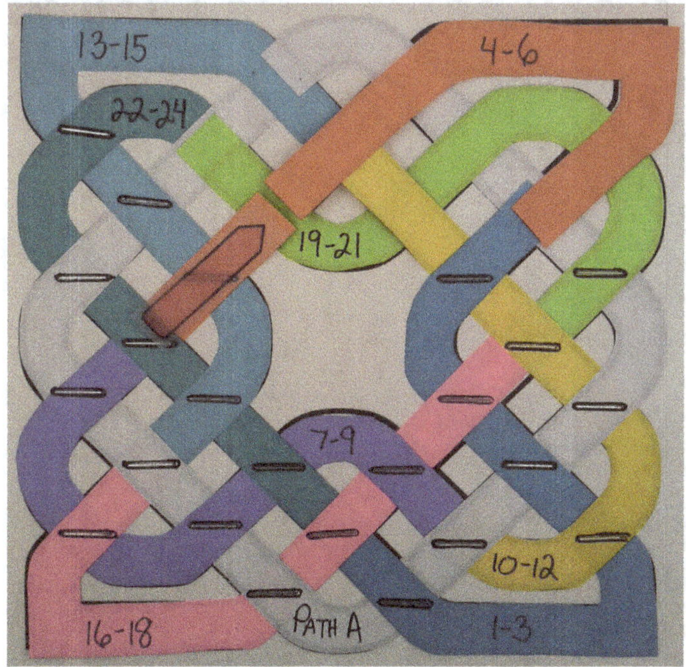

12. Lift right end of Path A out of the way. Position the cut section of Section 4-6 on the placement guide. Lay down Path A. Fasten path intersections where indicated.

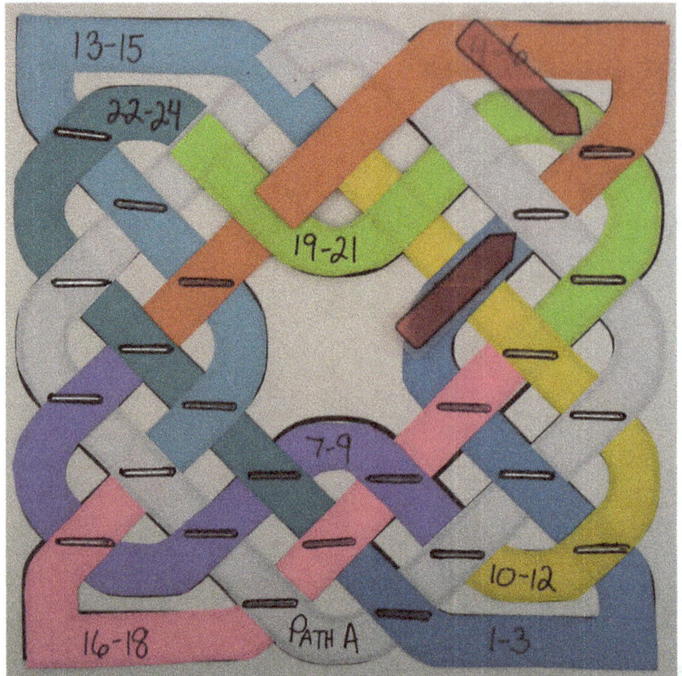

13. Lift Sections 10-12, 19-21, and Path A out of the way. Lay down Path A, tucking end under Section 13-15; then lay down Section 19-21, tucking end under Path A; and then lay down Section 10-12, tucking end under Section 4-6. Fasten path intersections where indicated.

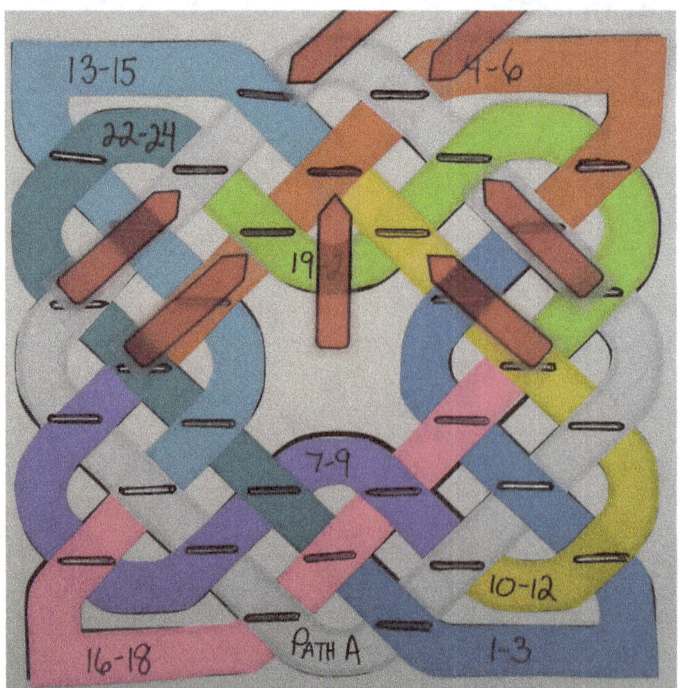

"Love is Love" Tracing Template

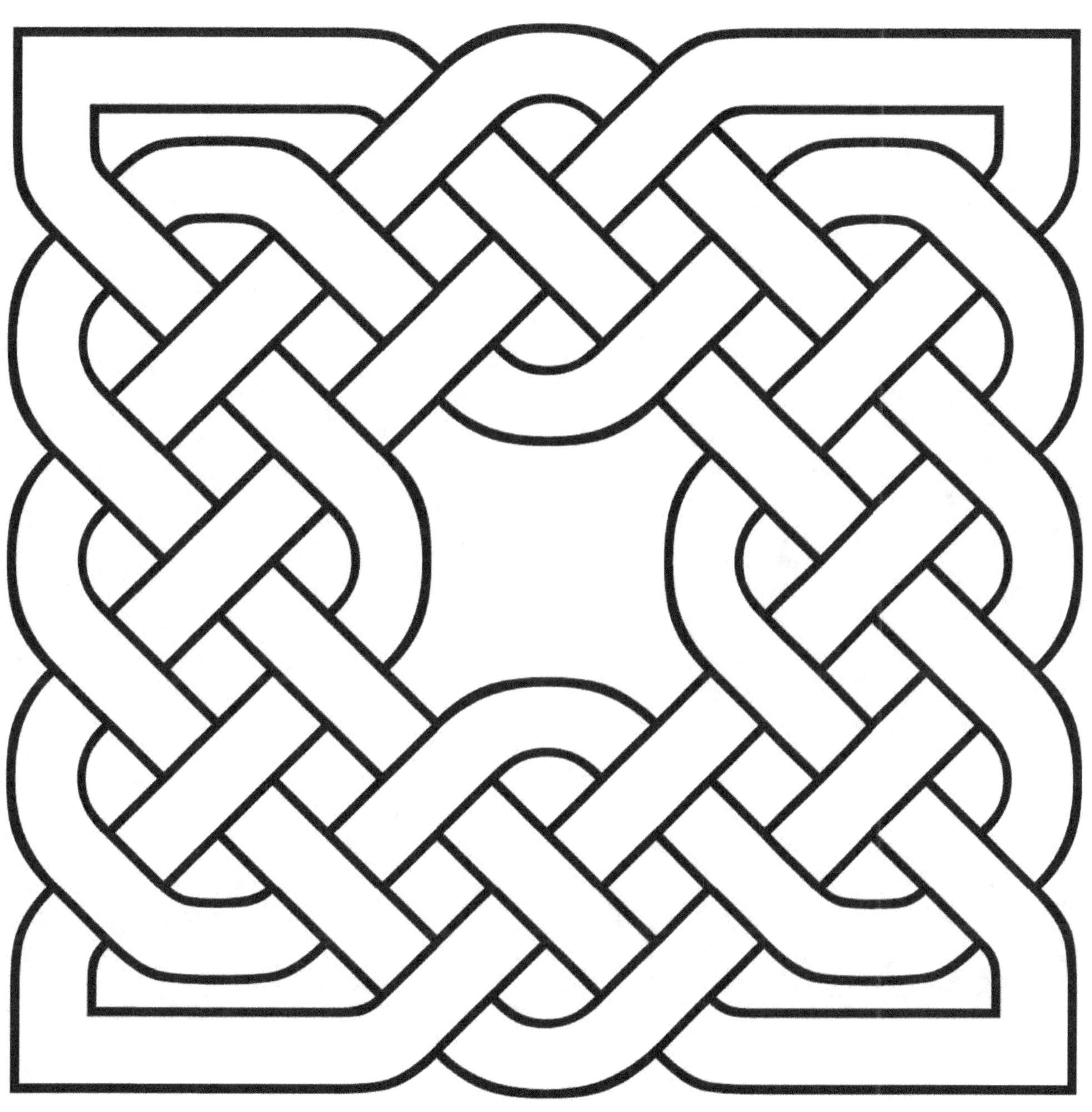

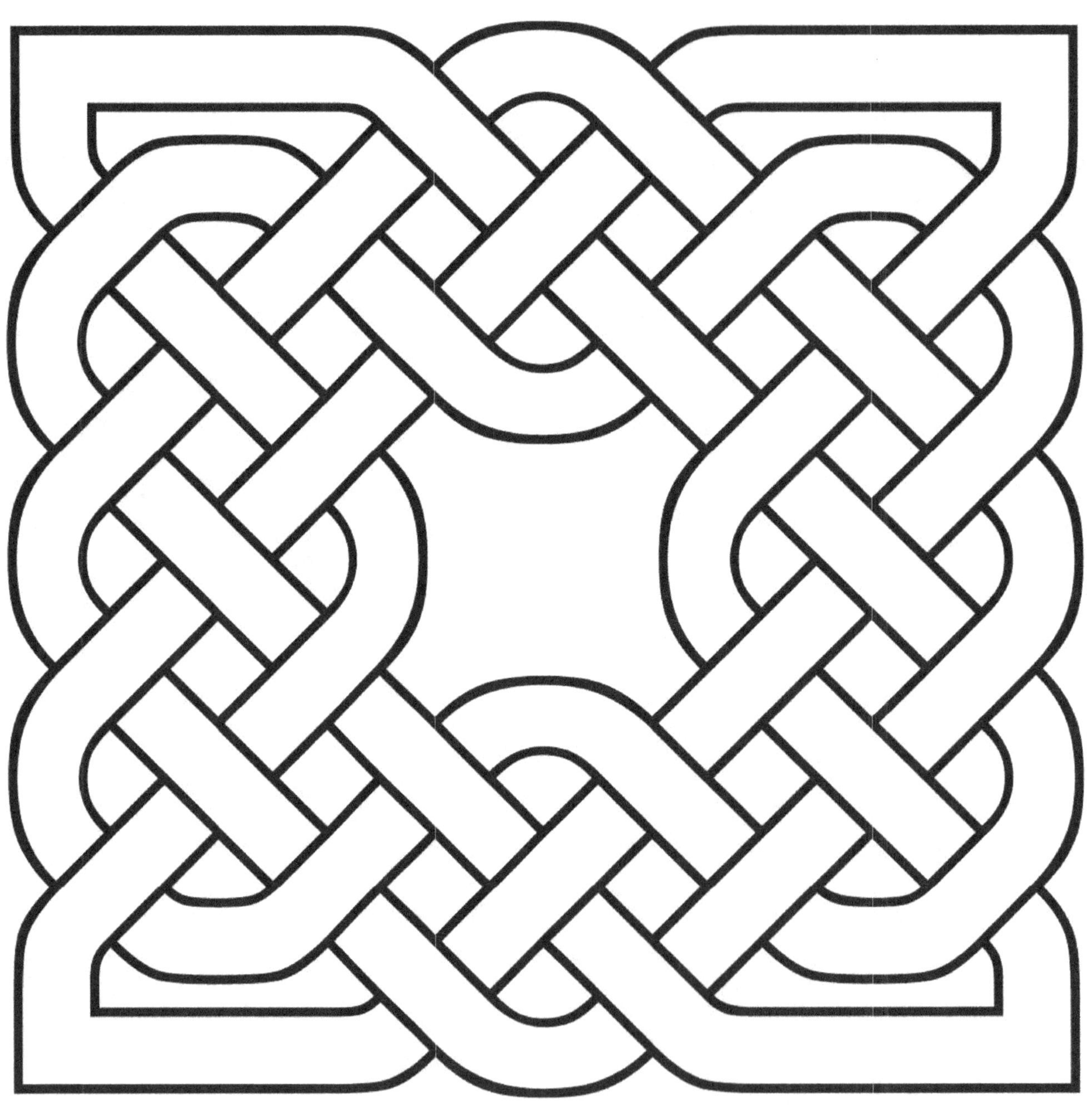

From the Author

I hope you have enjoyed this method of weaving Celtic knots. These are just the basics. Where you take it is up to you.

If you have any comments, questions, or feedback, please contact me at rkh@nachograndmasquilts.com.

Check out my website at http://nachograndmasquilts.com/about/.

Follow me on Facebook https://www.facebook.com/NachoGrandmasQuilts/ and Instagram: RaymondKHouston.

Thank you,
Raymond K. Houston

Did you love this book? Check out Raymond's first book, *Woven Celtic Knots* for more ways to create beautiful art.

Order online at

https://bluedragonpublishing.com/product/woven-celtic-knots/

or through your favorite bookstore.

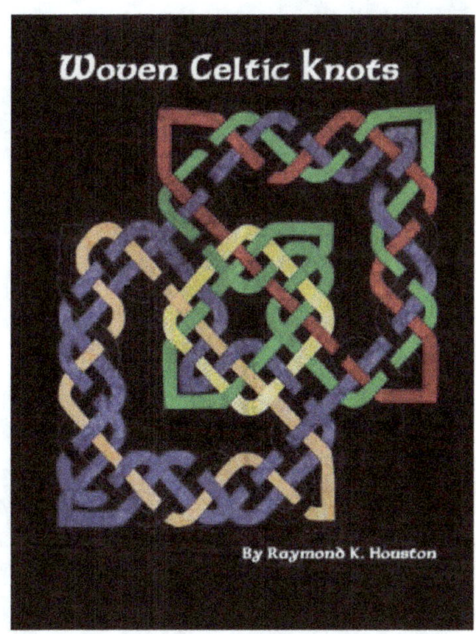

www.ingramcontent.com/pod-product-compliance
Lightning Source LLC
Chambersburg PA
CBHW080500030726
47592CB00011B/3192